Healthy Family Favorites

Mary Diederichs

MacMillan Books
P.O. Box 308
Kirkland, Washington 98083-0308

Cover illustration by Trina Sullivan
Design and layout by George Guy

First edition published: 2008 (MacMillan Books)

Library of Congress Catalogue Card Number: 2008929661
　　　　Diederichs, Mary
　　　　Healthy Family Favorites:
　　　　A Fresh Approach to Eating Great Food
　　　　First Edition: Includes index.

ISBN: 978-0-9818248-0-2

Every recipe in this book is designed to help readers make healthier choices about the food they eat. Healthy Family Favorites is intended as a reference and not medical advice. It is not intended to be a substitute for any treatment that has been prescribed by your medical practitioner. Anyone who suspects they have a medical problem should seek medical help.

Every recipe in this book has been adapted to fit a healthier lifestyle. If any recipe has previously been copyrighted, it is unintentional and without the author's knowledge.

ACKNOWLEDGMENTS

To Steve, Lisa and Daniel — my favorite food samplers.

The idea for this book was started by Steve Diederichs, my husband; and I thank him for encouraging me on this journey.

I owe a special gratitude to my mother, Jackie, who, in addition to sharing with me her love for cooking, also provided me with the talent and ability to cook. Thanks to Janet, my sister, for sharing her wonderful recipes and support. Many thanks to my family, friends and associates for tirelessly listening to me talk about my cookbook.

FOREWORD
by Alicia Guy

RECIPES PASSED ON from one generation to the next are a priceless treasure. Unassuming tin recipe boxes often hold the best record of a family's culinary history. I love looking through a family's collection of recipes as if it were a photo album. The formally handwritten recipes on faded index cards smudged with flour can reveal quite a portrait of the person who collected those recipes. Quickbreads were invented in a good year to address a bumper crop of zucchini. Side notes on a cake recipe reveal who likes nuts and who likes chocolate frosting. I marvel at the fact that these kitchen gems are often too easily discarded — destined for the rubbish bin after so many wooden spoons have told their stories time after time.

Mary Diederichs recognizes the worth of documenting some of her own culinary favorites. It is positively delightful to read this collection of recipes that brought joy and delicious meals to Mary's family. Four generations of Mary's family are represented — from the Ranger Cookies made by her Grandmother Biddy when Mary was a child, down to the Twice-Baked Potatoes made by her daughter, Lisa.

Best of all, Mary's collection is contemporary in its approach to taste and nutrition. With a focus on fresh vegetables, herbs and seafood, most of the recipes utilize low-fat cooking methods – ideal for anyone who is watching their weight or just wants to eat more healthfully. Even Grandma Biddy's cookies are made without shortening – a trans-fat ingredient that makes many generational baking recipes obsolete.

I hope many of Mary's meals make their way to your dinner table on a regular basis. And may your gatherings of family and friends in the kitchen and at the table also bring about pleasant memories.

T A B L E
O F
C O N T E N T S

INTRODUCTION............................8,9

HOW TO.................................10

HERB GARDEN 11

APPETIZERS..13

Barbecued Pork, 14

Bruschetta, 15

Deviled Eggs, 16

Shrimp Dip, 17

Smoked Salmon Spread, 18

Steamed Clams with Pesto Sauce, 19

Stuffed Mushrooms, 20

BREADS 21

Banana Nut Bread, 22

Blueberry Oat Bran Muffins, 23

Fruit and Pumpkin Seed Bars, 24

Graham Bread, 25

Sweet Corn Bread, 26

Zucchini Carrot Bread, 27

SALADS.....................................29

Blue Cheese Dressing, 30

Caprese Chop Salad, 31

Chicken Curry Salad, 32

Chinese Egg Noodles with Shrimp, 33

SALADS.....................................(continued)

Fresh Pear and Gorgonzola Salad, 34

Sweet Potato Salad, 35

Roasted Beet Salad, 36

Seafood Cobb Salad, 37

Shrimp Corkscrew Salad, 38

Spinach Salad with Chicken, 39

Strawberry Spinach Salad, 40

Taco Salad, 41

Vinaigrette, 42

SOUPS......................................43

Chicken Noodle Soup, 44

Chicken Stock, 45

Minestrone Soup, 46

Pumpkin Soup, 47

Seafood Stew, 48

Tomato Basil Soup, 50

SLOW COOKER..................................51

Chicken with Celery Root and Garlic, 52

Southwest Chicken Chili, 53

Irish Lamb Stew, 54

Pork Roast with Sauerkraut, 55

Pot Roast and Gravy, 56

TABLE
OF
CONTENTS

ENTRÉES..57

Chicken with Fresh Mozzarella
and Noodles, 58

Chili, 59

Cracker-................Crumb Pork Chops, 60

Enchiladas, 61

Roast Chicken with Garlic, 62

Roast Chicken with Citrus, 63

Hamburgers – Mary's Style, 64

Paprika Chicken and Gravy, 65

Italian Meatballs, 66

Joe's Special, 67

Lamb Shish Kebab, 68

Marinara Sauce, 69

Marinated Flank Steak, 70

One-Pot Italian Sausage and Potatoes, 71

Pork Tenderloin, 72

Quiche, 73

Roast Turkey, 74

Dressing for Roast Turkey, 75

Stuffed Red Peppers, 76

Swedish Meatballs, 77

Chicken Stir Fry with Peanut Sauce, 78

Turkey Meatloaf, 79

SEAFOOD..81

Baked Lemon Salmon, 82

Grilled Salmon, 83

Halibut with Fresh Herbs, 84

Halibut with Panko Breading, 85

Oven-Baked Fish, 86

Prawns with Cilantro and Lime, 87

Rosemary Garlic Prawns, 88

Salmon in White Wine, 89

Salmon with Garlic Paste, 90

Sea Scallops with Lime, 91

Sole with Capers and Olives, 92

Soy-Ginger Salmon, 93

Tilapia with Rosemary-Ginger Rub, 94

VEGETABLES..95

Acorn Squash, 96

Artichokes with Yogurt Dipping Sauce, 97

Caramelized Mushrooms
in White Wine, 98

Cauliflower Mash, 99

Fall Harvest Green Beans, 100

Italian Zucchini Bake, 101

Lemon Asparagus, 102

Roasted Butternut Squash, 103

Roasted Cauliflower with Olives, 104

TABLE OF CONTENTS

VEGETABLES......................... (continued)

   Roasted Tomatoes, 105

   Sautéed Beet Greens, 106

   Sesame Spinach, 107

   Spinach with Balsamic Vinegar, 108

   Swiss Chard, 109

   Vegetable Stir Fry, 110

   Zucchini and Green Chiles, 111

   Zucchini Stir Fry, 112

SAUCES................................. **113**

   Applesauce, 114

   Pesto, 115

   Secret Sauce, 116

   Sour Cream Sauce with Capers, 117

   Tartar Sauce, 118

   Yogurt Dipping Sauce, 118

SIDES...................................... **119**

   Bhutanese Red Rice Pilaf, 120

   Black-Eyed Peas, 121

   *Mashed Yams with Rosemary
   and Toasted Hazelnuts, 122*

   Oven-Baked Potato Wedges, 123

   Roasted Potatoes, 124

   Scalloped Potatoes, 125

SIDES... (continued)

   Sweet Potato Casserole, 126

   Twice-Baked Potatoes, 127

   White Beans with Rosemary, 128

   Brown Rice with Dressing, 129

DESSERTS.. **131**

   Apple Walnut Cobbler, 132

   Brownies, 133

   *Carrot Cake with Cream Cheese
   Frosting, 134*

   Cheese and Fruit Platter, 135

   Coconut Angel Cake, 136

   Fresh Berry Coffee Cake, 137

   Iced Pumpkin Cookies, 138

   Pumpkin Pudding, 139

   Ranger Cookies, 140

   Wild Blackberry Cobbler, 141

INDEX... **142**

INTRODUCTION

I COME FROM A FOOD-FOCUSED FAMILY. My mother was a very creative cook, and she made food an important part of our birthdays, holidays, and nightly dinners. I remember catching the passion for cooking around the age of 10 when presented with the opportunity to prepare dinner for my family. I willingly accepted the challenge; and with this choice, my life would be forever changed. My first meal was a pot roast dinner with potatoes and carrots, my favorite. My introduction into the world of cooking was now complete. I was hooked.

Birthdays, as in many homes, were very special meals for my family growing up. It was a tradition in our house that when it was your birthday, you were able to choose the menu. Even as a child, I was attracted to old-fashioned favorites. I always seemed to pick pot roast. I loved the marriage of tastes and texture of this dish, from the tender, moist beef to the colorful earthy vegetables. The flavorful rich gravy finished the dish. The process of cooking this meal was so much fun, from searing the beef in our cast-iron skillet to slow-roasting it in the oven for hours. Everything always came out perfectly; and by the time it was done, I was so hungry from all the good smells. It is such a satisfying meal. Every birthday ended with Coconut Angel Cake, a recipe my mom discovered. I make it now for special occasions.

Like birthdays, our nightly dinners were also a time of celebration. We enjoyed experimenting with new recipes and challenging our culinary knowledge as we helped one another create delicious meals. Everyone in my family is a fabulous cook, so this made those times even more exciting. Each person added their own interpretation and input into the courses being served. My mother, being the talented cook she was, often made wonderful soups for us to try. My husband's Grandmother, Pat, was well known for her roasted chicken – a wonderful treat we frequently had the privilege of sharing. My Aunt Jane's Chicken Curry Salad was such a hit that it became a staple food served at every baby and bridal shower.

INTRODUCTION

FOR ME, COOKING FOR LOVED ONES is the best gift I could ever give. I find great joy in sharing my passion for food and find cooking to be therapeutic not only for me, but for many people I speak with. I love educating people on alternative ways of preparing meals and enjoy the reactions when they find out that what I cook is focused on being delicious and healthy. You don't have to sacrifice taste to eat healthy; you just have to be creative and experiment in knowing how to bring out the flavor in food. My biggest thrill, though, is sharing my recipes with my two children and husband, and inviting them to cook alongside me.

I have been cooking since the age of 10, starting with my first pot roast , and I've continued to collect and improve upon recipes that I have received from friends and family over the years. I have had the good fortune during the past few years to travel with my husband around the world on business and to experience food from different cultures. I have encountered wonderful opportunities to learn about the methods of cooking and the ingredients that go into the foods. I have incorporated some of these foods and methods into the recipes in this book and I believe you will find them to be delicious.

My goal with this book is to show you how easy it is to take the food you grew up with and make it satisfying and also good for you, too. We make choices every day about the food we eat. The recipes in this book show you how simple it is to eat healthy and how rewarding the cooking experience can be for you and your loved ones. *Healthy Family Favorites* is a collection of recipes I've created to feed my family. They are based on using the freshest ingredients available, with low sugar and high fiber content. I've added some easy cooking techniques and suggestions to help you plan your meals. I hope these become your family favorites, too.

Mary

H O W   T O

THROUGHOUT THIS BOOK, you will occasionally run across the () symbol, either in the ingredients list or the recipe directions. These icons will point you to tricks or tips I've included to help to make these easy recipes even easier.

E X A M P L E

HOW TO TOAST WALNUTS

- Toasting the walnuts brings out their flavor.

- Place them in a dry fry pan over medium to medium-high heat and stir frequently, about 5 minutes.

- Be sure to watch them so they don't burn. Adjust the heat as needed.

Herb Garden

Fresh herbs are a great way to make a dish taste better. They flavor the food well when you are cutting back on fat, sugar and salt. You can pick them up at the grocery store or plant your own.

Herb Garden

I use fresh herbs whenever possible. I plant them in the spring and enjoy them throughout most of the year.

1 6-inch x 3-foot planter box
   (not all containers have drainage
   holes, so drill some if necessary)
5 4-inch potted herbs:
   basil, Italian parsley, lemon thyme,
   purple sage, chives, or cilantro
Nasturtium seeds
Potting soil
Gravel
Fertilizer

PLANTER BOX

You can leave the box plain or paint it.

Paint or spray the box with an oil-base primer. Let dry and paint with a latex paint.

Cover the base of the pot with gravel.

Add enough soil to reach halfway up the planter.

Remove the herbs from their pots, loosen their roots, and place the herbs into the soil, spacing them 5-6 inches apart. Add more soil and gently pat the soil down to secure the plants.

Place the germinated nasturtium seeds around the herbs.

Water the herbs and keep them wet for 30 days after planting.

Fertilize with half-strength fertilizer once a week.

HOW TO GERMINATE SEEDS

- Place the seeds in 2 wet paper towels.

- Keep towels damp for 3-5 days. The seeds should start to sprout.

- Nasturtium flowers are edible and they are so pretty in a salad.

Appetizers

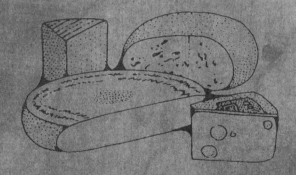

Simple and elegant, appetizers are good with drinks or as part of a dinner menu. Keep them simple and remember to make your presentation pretty. We eat with our eyes first.

Barbecued Pork

—MAKES 8 SERVINGS—

*I don't remember where this recipe came from, but I do know that
every time I bring it to a party, it's one of the first plates to go.*

PORK

1 pound pork tenderloin
1 teaspoon dry mustard
½ teaspoon fresh thyme
⅛ teaspoon sea salt

MARINADE

3 tablespoons dry sherry
3 tablespoons light soy sauce
1 clove garlic, minced fine
1 teaspoon fresh ginger, grated
½ teaspoon fresh thyme

GLAZE

3 tablespoons raspberry jelly
½ teaspoon light soy sauce
½ teaspoon dry sherry

HOT MUSTARD SAUCE

2 tablespoons Coleman's mustard
2-3 teaspoons water or beer
⅛ teaspoon salt

Mix together to desired consistency.

Place the pork on a piece of plastic wrap.

In a small bowl, combine the mustard, thyme and sea salt. Rub over the pork.

In another small bowl, mix the sherry, soy sauce, garlic, ginger and thyme.
Pour into a Ziploc bag. Place the pork into the bag and refrigerate 3 hours.

Preheat oven to 350°F.

Spray an ovenproof baking dish with nonstick cooking spray. Place the meat
and the marinade into the prepared dish and bake 50-60 minutes, turning meat
over once. Remove pork to another pan.

In a small bowl, combine the jelly, soy and sherry. Spread this over the meat
and let sit for 1 hour.

Mix mustard, water and salt together in a small bowl.

Slice the meat into ¼-inch rounds and serve on a platter with hot mustard,
ketchup and toasted sesame seeds in little serving bowls.

Bruschetta

1 sliced baguette
1 pound fresh mozzarella, sliced
Fresh garlic, pressed

Toast the baguette slices and rub the top of each piece with fresh garlic.

Place a slice of fresh mozzarella on top of the garlic toast.

Arrange these on a cookie sheet and melt the cheese under the broiler.

Put a spoonful of the tomato mixture on top.

TOPPING

4 ripe Roma tomatoes, washed, deseeded and diced
$\frac{1}{2}$ clove garlic, pressed
2 tablespoons finely chopped red onion
6 basil leaves, torn into tiny pieces
$\frac{1}{8}$ teaspoon dried oregano
1 tablespoon extra-virgin olive oil
Salt and pepper to taste

In a medium bowl, combine the above ingredients.

Serve with sliced baguettes, tortilla chips or toasted bagels.

HOW TO DESEED TOMATOES

- Cut the tomato in half.
- Cut each half into three equal wedges.
- Use a small sharp knife to cut under the seeds, close to the flesh, from one end of the wedge to the other.
- Remove and discard seeds.
- Slice or dice flesh as required.

Deviled Eggs

—MAKES 6 SERVINGS—

This recipe has always been a family favorite as long as I can remember. My husband's family always serves these at their gatherings. They're easy to prepare ahead, and they dress up to impress everyone at the party.

6 hard-boiled eggs, cooled and cut in half
¼ cup reduced-fat mayonnaise
2 teaspoons fresh lemon juice
Salt and pepper, to taste
Chopped tomatoes, sliced black olives or capers
Spinach leaves

Gently scoop out the yolks and place them in a medium bowl.

Stir in the mayonnaise, lemon juice, salt and pepper to taste.

Set each egg white half on a spinach leaf and fill with the yolk mixture.

Decorate the tops with chopped tomatoes, black olives or capers.

HARD-BOILED EGGS

6 large fresh eggs

Place the eggs in a medium saucepan.

Cover with cold water. The water should be one inch higher than the eggs.

Cover with a lid. Bring to a boil over high heat.

When the water boils, remove the pan from the heat. Let the eggs sit, covered, for 15 minutes.

Drain the hot water and immediately run cold water over the eggs.

Shake the pan gently to crack the eggshells.

Continue running cold water over the eggs until the water stays cold.

Peel the eggs immediately.

A P P E T I Z E R S

Shrimp Dip

—MAKES 8 SERVINGS—

1 8-ounce package fat-free cream
   cheese, room temperature
¼ cup reduced-fat mayonnaise
¼ cup fat-free plain yogurt
3 tablespoons chili sauce
2 teaspoons lemon juice
½ teaspoon lemon zest
1 teaspoon grated onion
¼ teaspoon Worcestershire sauce
1 cup salad shrimp, chopped

HOW TO GRATE AN ONION

- Grate a sweet onion with a box grater over a piece of wax paper.

Mix all the ingredients except the salad shrimp in a blender.

Remove the mixture to a serving bowl and stir in the shrimp, reserving a few to decorate the top.

Refrigerate for up to 24 hours.

Serve with crackers, vegetables or sliced French bread.

Smoked Salmon Spread

*I first discovered this recipe a year ago when I was traveling in Alaska.
A plate of rolls and this colorful spread were brought to our table.
I couldn't wait to try it. I took a bite and was surprised by its interesting
blend of flavors. I went home and recreated this dish. I like to serve it
with fresh vegetables and crackers. It's great on an antipasto plate.*

½ cup light cream cheese, room temperature
¾ cup smoked salmon, shredded into small pieces
2 tablespoons toasted walnuts, chopped fine
1 teaspoon fresh lemon juice
¼ teaspoon lemon zest
1 teaspoon chopped fresh dill weed
1 tablespoon chopped fresh flat leaf parsley
1 teaspoon prepared horseradish

Combine all ingredients in a medium bowl.

Mix with a fork until blended.

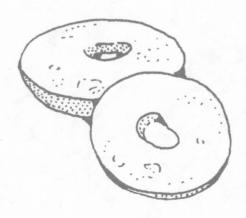

Steamed Clams with Pesto Sauce

*Present this dish in a large serving bowl either as an appetizer
or as a main course. Serve with crusty French bread and a green salad.*

1 14.5-ounce can diced tomatoes with basil
½ cup pesto — store-bought is fine or make your own
½ teaspoon salt
Fresh ground pepper, to taste
1 tablespoon butter
1 tablespoon canola oil
2 green onions, finely chopped
1 clove garlic, minced
3 tablespoons fresh Italian parsley, chopped
½ cup dry white wine
2 pounds Manila clams, cleaned

In a medium saucepan, combine the tomatoes, pesto,
salt and pepper.

Bring to a boil, reduce the heat to medium and cook until ⅓ of the liquid has
evaporated.

Heat a large frying pan over medium-high heat.

Add the butter, oil, green onion, and salt and pepper to taste.

Cook for 2 minutes.

Add the garlic and cook for 1 minute.

Add the parsley, wine and clams.

Reduce the heat to low and cover with a lid.

Steam for approximately 5-8 minutes or until the shells open.

Agitate the pan during this time to cook the clams evenly.

Stir in the tomato-basil mixture.

Stuffed Mushrooms

—MAKES 4 SERVINGS—

Try using different mushrooms — Crimini or Portobello would work well. A large earthy platter with an assortment would make an impressive presentation. Accent the dish with fresh herbs.

1 pound Italian chicken sausage
1 pound large cap white mushrooms

Preheat oven to 350°F.

Clean the mushrooms and remove the stems.

Stuff the sausage into the mushroom caps and place on a cookie sheet.

Bake for 30 minutes or until the sausage is done.

Serve hot.

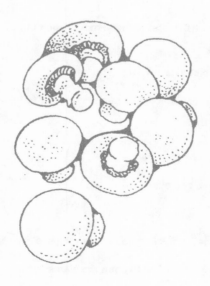

Breads

Breads are an excellent way to get fiber into your diet. Whole-grain flours contain more fiber than white flour, as illustrated below:

Per 1/4 cup flour {
White:	1 gram
Graham:	3 grams
Whole-wheat:	4 grams
Oat:	3 grams
Spelt:	4 grams

Banana Nut Bread

—MAKES 1 BREAD LOAF OR 3 MINI-LOAVES—

When using glass pans for baking, set the temperature 25° lower than specified. Glass heats faster than metal and holds the heat longer.
(Colorado Cache Cookbook)

1 cup mashed banana, about 3 medium
½ cup unsweetened applesauce
½ cup granulated sugar
⅓ cup fat-free milk, fat-free half and
   half or low-fat buttermilk
2 eggs
1 teaspoon vanilla
2 ⅓ cups oat flour
1 teaspoon ground cinnamon
½ teaspoon allspice
1 teaspoon baking soda
½ teaspoon salt
½ cup chopped toasted walnuts

HOW TO TOAST WALNUTS

- Toasting the walnuts brings out their flavor.

- Place them in a dry fry pan over medium to medium-high heat and stir frequently, about 5 minutes.

- Be sure to watch them so they don't burn. Adjust the heat as needed.

Preheat oven to 350°F.

Spray loaf pans with nonstick cooking spray.

In a small bowl, mash the bananas with the back of a fork.

In a large bowl, mix together the applesauce, sugar, milk, eggs and vanilla. Add the mashed bananas and blend.

Add the oat flour, cinnamon, allspice, soda and salt. Fold in the nuts.

Pour batter into prepared pans and bake until a toothpick inserted into the center of the bread comes out clean — about 35 minutes for small loaves, 45-55 minutes for a bread loaf pan.

Transfer pans to a rack to cool for 10 minutes, then turn bread out onto the rack.

Blueberry Oat Bran Muffins

—MAKES 12-16 MUFFINS—

Spelt flour can be used in many of the same ways as white and whole-wheat flour. It has more fiber and doesn't seem to cause as many problems in those people who are sensitive to wheat.

2 cups crushed oat bran flakes

1/3 cup flax seed, finely ground (a coffee grinder works great)

1 2/3 cups nonfat milk

4 egg whites, slightly beaten

1 tablespoon vanilla

2 cups spelt or oat flour

1/2 cup brown sugar

2 teaspoons baking powder

1 1/2 teaspoons baking soda

1/8 teaspoon salt

1 1/2 teaspoons ground cinnamon

2 cups fresh or frozen blueberries (raspberries can be substituted)

Preheat the oven to 400°F.

Spray muffin tins with nonstick cooking spray.

In a medium bowl, combine the crushed oat bran flakes, ground flax seeds, milk, egg whites and vanilla.

In a large bowl, combine the flour, brown sugar, baking powder, baking soda, salt and cinnamon. Add the cereal mixture to this and blend. Do not overmix. Fold in the berries. Let batter sit for 10 minutes if using spelt flour.

Spoon batter into the prepared cups, filling them 2/3 full.

Bake for 20 minutes or until done. Test by placing a toothpick in the middle; it should come out clean.

Fruit and Pumpkin Seed Bars

—MAKES 12 BARS—

I eat these bars for both snacks and dessert.

1 cup whole-wheat or spelt flour
2/3 cup rolled oats
1/3 cup flax meal
1 2.25-ounce jar baby prunes
1/2 cup chopped golden raisins
1/2 cup chopped dried cranberries
1/2 cup chopped toasted pumpkin seeds
1/4 cup chopped toasted sesame seeds
1/3 cup water

Preheat the oven to 325°F.

Lightly spray a 9x9-inch pan with nonstick baking spray.

In a cast iron skillet or frying pan, toast the pumpkin seeds and sesame seeds until light brown. Cool and chop.

In a large mixing bowl, combine the flour, oats, flax meal, prunes, raisins, cranberries, seeds and water. With a large spoon or damp hands, mix until blended.

With damp hands, press the mixture into the prepared pan. Precut the bars slightly with a sharp knife.

Bake for 25-30 minutes or until done. The mixture should still be soft in the middle.

Cool on a rack and cut into bars.

Store in the refrigerator.

Graham Bread

If you don't have buttermilk, fat-free milk will work by adding
2 tablespoons regular vinegar to the milk. If you use spelt flour,
let the batter sit for 10 minutes before you put the bread into the oven.

2 teaspoons baking soda
2 cups low-fat buttermilk
1 cup white, whole-wheat or spelt flour
2 cups graham flour
½ cup sugar
1 teaspoon salt

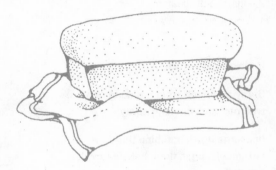

Preheat oven to 400°F.

Spray the bread pans with nonstick cooking spray.

In a large bowl, whisk together the buttermilk and soda. The milk will foam.

In a medium bowl, stir together the two flours, sugar and salt.

Combine the flour mixture into the milk and stir until blended.

Pour into 1 bread pan or 3 mini-loaf pans.

Bake for 30 minutes for the mini-loaf pans or 45 minutes for the bread pan.

Bread is done when toothpick placed in the center comes out clean.

Let the pans sit on a cooling rack for 10 minutes.

Remove bread from the pan and let it cool before slicing.

Sweet Corn Bread

—MAKES 9 BARS—

This is perfect served with chili or soup on a cold winter night.

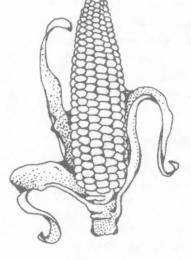

½ cup cornmeal
½ cup sugar
1 ½ cups oat flour
1 tablespoon baking powder
½ teaspoon salt
2 tablespoons canola oil
½ cup plus 1 tablespoon flax meal
2 eggs, slightly beaten
1 ¼ cups fat-free milk

Preheat oven to 350°F.

Spray an 8-inch square baking pan with nonstick cooking spray.

In a large bowl, combine the cornmeal, sugar, flour, baking powder and salt.

In a medium bowl, combine the oil, flax meal, eggs and milk. Lightly stir and then add to the flour mixture.

Stir until blended. Do not overmix.

Pour batter into prepared pan.

Bake for 40 minutes or until a toothpick placed in the center comes out clean.

Let sit for 10 minutes and cut into squares.

Zucchini Carrot Bread

You can substitute up to half the butter or fat in your recipes with unsweetened applesauce, as I have done with this recipe.

1 egg
2 egg whites
1/3 cup unsweetened applesauce
2 tablespoons canola oil
2/3 cup sugar
1 teaspoon vanilla
1/2 cup grated carrot
1/2 cup grated zucchini

1 1/2 cups spelt flour*, oat flour or
   whole-wheat pastry flour
1/2 teaspoon baking soda
1/2 teaspoon baking powder
1 1/2 teaspoons ground cinnamon
1/2 teaspoon salt
1/2 cup chopped walnuts

Preheat oven to 325°F.

Spray one loaf pan or 2 mini-loaf pans with nonstick cooking spray.

In a large bowl, beat the eggs until light and fluffy, about one minute. Add the applesauce, oil, sugar, vanilla, carrot and zucchini. Mix lightly.

Add the flour, baking soda, baking powder, cinnamon and salt to the zucchini mixture and stir until blended. Fold in nuts.

Pour batter into the prepared pans.

Bake for 40-45 minutes for the small pans, or 55-60 for the bread loaf pan. Bread is done when a toothpick placed in the center comes out clean.

Remove pans from the oven and let sit on a cooling rack for 10 minutes.

Remove bread from the pans and cool on the rack.

* If using spelt flour, let batter sit for 10 minutes before placing it in the oven.

Salads

The salad can be a light meal or part of a larger meal.
Its ability to offer fresh vegetables or fruit makes it a
healthy dish.

Blue Cheese Dressing

— MAKES 1 CUP —

⅓ cup low-fat mayonnaise

¼ cup fat-free plain yogurt

2 tablespoons light sour cream

3-4 tablespoons nonfat milk

½ teaspoon fresh lemon juice

1 teaspoon Dijon mustard

Dash cayenne pepper

⅓ cup crumbled blue cheese (Maytag, Rogue Creamery, Smokey Blue)

Combine all the ingredients in a medium bowl.

Mix with the back of a fork until blended.

Add more milk if needed.

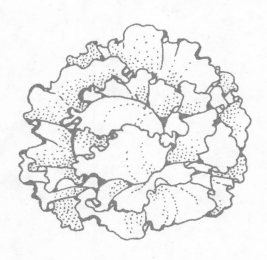

Caprese Chop Salad

—MAKES 4 SERVINGS—

I had an Insalata Caprese every day when I was in Italy.
It is one of the simplest of salads, requiring the freshest vine-ripened
tomatoes found only during summer. This salad recreates those
wonderful tastes in an easy-to-make everyday dish.

1 head romaine lettuce, chopped into bite-size pieces
¼ cup chopped red onion
2 tomatoes, chopped
10-12 kalamata olives, chopped
½ cup fresh mozzarella cheese, cut into small pieces
¼ cup fresh basil, chopped
Balsamic vinaigrette (page 42)
Large chilled salad bowl

Place the romaine, onion, tomatoes, olives, cheese and basil into the bowl.

Toss with the balsamic vinaigrette.

Chicken Curry Salad

—MAKES 8 SERVINGS—

Serve this salad on individual chilled salad plates. Place a large spoonful of salad on a Bibb lettuce leaf. Scatter a few almonds on top. Try using chopped apples instead of grapes.

½ cup fat-free yogurt
½ cup low-fat mayonnaise
1 ½ teaspoons apple cider vinegar
1 ½ teaspoons curry powder
1 ½ teaspoons light soy sauce
4 cups cooked chicken breast, cut into
   bite-size pieces
1 5-ounce can sliced water chestnuts, lightly
   chopped
1 pound red or green grapes, cut in half lengthwise
1 11-ounce can mandarin oranges, drained
1 cup chopped celery with leaves
½ cup toasted slivered almonds

In a small bowl, combine the yogurt, mayonnaise, vinegar, curry powder and soy sauce. Mix until blended.

In a large bowl, add the chicken, water chestnuts, grapes, mandarin oranges, and celery. Mix lightly.

Chill until ready to use.

Toss the dressing over the chicken mixture right before serving.

Sprinkle the slivered almonds on top.

Chinese Egg Noodles with Shrimp

—MAKES 6 SERVINGS—

This salad is always popular at our family reunions.

8-ounce package Rose brand Chinese Egg Noodles, cut in half
½ cup low-fat mayonnaise
½ cup nonfat yogurt
1 tablespoon yellow mustard
1 tablespoon cider vinegar
1 tablespoon extra virgin olive oil
2 teaspoons Johnny's Seasoning Salt
½ teaspoon fresh ground pepper
½ cup sliced green onions
1 cup finely chopped celery with leaves
1 cup salad shrimp

Cook the noodles as directed.

Rinse with cold water and drain.

In a large serving bowl, combine the mayonnaise, yogurt, prepared mustard, vinegar, oil, salt, pepper, green onions, celery and shrimp.

Chill before serving.

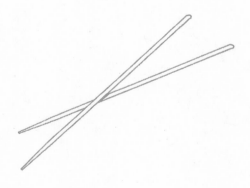

Fresh Pear and Gorgonzola Salad

—MAKES 6 SERVINGS—

This salad is delicious and a wonderful start to any meal. The pear and toasted walnuts add an interesting taste to this unique salad.

4 cups romaine lettuce, cut into bite-size pieces
¼ cup chopped red onion
¼ cup chopped red pepper
½ cup apple, cut into ½-inch pieces
1 ripe pear, sliced thin
½ cup crumbled Gorgonzola cheese (Blue Gorgonzola Mountain Ciresa)
½ cup toasted walnuts
Raspberry vinaigrette (page 42)

Place the lettuce, onion, red pepper and apple into a chilled salad bowl.

Toss the salad with the raspberry vinaigrette and candied walnuts.

Place the sliced pear and the cheese decoratively on top.

Sweet Potato Salad

This purple salad was served to us at Cafe Pesto in Hilo, Hawaii. The color comes from the Okinawa sweet potato. The skin is brown, but the inside is purple. If you can't find this, try using a different variety of sweet potato.

2 medium Okinawa sweet potatoes (available at some Asian grocery stores)
6 medium Yukon Gold potatoes
2 tablespoons salt
1 cup nonfat plain yogurt
1/2 cup reduced-fat mayonnaise
1 1/2 tablespoons Dijon mustard
1 tablespoon fresh dill, finely chopped
1 teaspoon fresh parsley, finely chopped
6 hard-boiled eggs, chopped
6 scallions, finely chopped
Salt and fresh ground pepper to taste
1/3 cup Rogue Creamery blue cheese, crumbled

Place the potatoes and salt in a large pot of water. Bring the water to a boil, then lower the heat and simmer for 10 to 15 minutes, until the potatoes are barely tender when pierced with a knife.

Drain the potatoes in a colander.

When cool, peel the sweet potatoes.

Place the potatoes in the refrigerator to cool.

In a medium bowl, combine the yogurt, mayonnaise, mustard, dill, salt and pepper.

Cut up the cooled potatoes and place them in a large serving bowl. Add the eggs and scallions. Gently fold the dressing into the potato mixture. Salt and pepper to taste.

Refrigerate for 4-6 hours.

Just before serving, sprinkle the cheese over the salad.

Roasted Beet Salad

—MAKES 6 SERVINGS—

Beet lovers will enjoy this colorful salad.
The walnuts can be toasted days ahead.

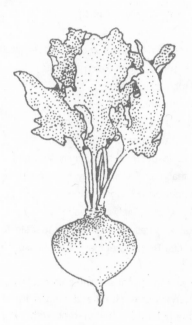

1 head romaine lettuce, washed and cut
   into bite-size pieces
¼ cup red onion, thinly sliced
½ cup roasted beets, cut into ¾-inch bites
⅓ cup toasted walnuts
½ cup crumbled blue cheese

**Place the romaine in a chilled
salad bowl.**

Add the onion and toss.

**Decorate the top with the beets,
walnuts and cheese.**

**Dress with raspberry vinaigrette (page 42)
or blue cheese dressing (page 30).**

TOASTED WALNUTS

1 cup walnut halves

**Place a medium frying pan over
medium-high heat.**

**Add the walnuts and cook until they
are light brown, stirring constantly.**

Reduce heat as needed.

ROASTED BEETS

4 2-inch beets, cleaned and trimmed

**Do not cut off the tail, but trim the
greens to 1 inch.**

Preheat the oven to 400°F.

**Place the beets in an ovenproof dish
with ½ cup water in the bottom.**

**Cover with aluminum foil and bake
for 1 hour.**

Cool, peel and slice.

Seafood Cobb Salad

—MAKES 4 SERVINGS—

*I ordered this in Juneau, Alaska, at the Twisted Fish Restaurant.
It's a wonderful main dish salad to enjoy when crab is in season.*

1 head romaine lettuce, clean and cut into bite-size pieces
1 tomato, sliced
1/4 cup red onion, chopped
1/2 pound crabmeat
1/2 pound salad shrimp
3/4 pound salmon, tilapia or halibut, cooked with Rosemary-Ginger Spice Rub
   (I use Stubb's brand)
1/2 lemon, cut into 4 slices
1 ripe avocado, cubed
1/4 cup blue cheese, crumbled
1/4 cup bacon bits

Place the lettuce, tomato and red onion on a large chilled serving platter.

Top with the crab, shrimp, fish, lemon, avocado, blue cheese and bacon bits.

Serve with blue cheese dressing (page 30) or secret sauce (page 116).

Shrimp Corkscrew Salad

—MAKES 8 SERVINGS—

I learned the recipe for this salad from my sister Sue many years ago at one of her Christmas parties. Ever since then, it has been a favorite of our family.

1 pound radiatore noodles
1 cup peas
1 cup finely chopped celery
½ cup finely chopped red onion
½ cup chopped red bell pepper
1 cup cubed Swiss cheese
1 pound salad shrimp

DRESSING

1 cup reduced-fat mayonnaise
   or ½ cup reduced-fat mayonnaise
   plus ½ cup nonfat plain yogurt
2 tablespoons apple cider vinegar
1 tablespoon fresh dill weed,
   or 1 teaspoon dried
Salt and pepper, to taste

Cook the noodles as directed. Rinse in cold water and drain.

Meanwhile, in a medium bowl, combine the mayonnaise, apple cider vinegar, dill weed, salt and pepper.

In a large serving bowl, combine the noodles, peas, celery, red onion, red pepper, Swiss cheese and shrimp.

Fold in the dressing and chill.

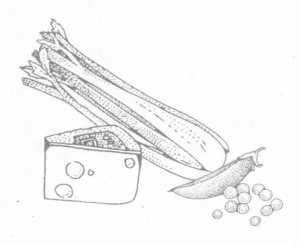

Spinach Salad with Chicken

—MAKES 4 SERVINGS—

This colorful salad complements any main course.

10 ounces fresh baby spinach

4 scallions, thinly sliced

1 cup cherry tomatoes, cut in half

½ cup sliced mushrooms

2 boneless chicken breasts, cooked, chilled and cut into bite-size pieces

½ cup crumbled blue cheese

¼ cup toasted slivered almonds

Salt and pepper, to taste

Balsamic vinaigrette (page 42)

In a large bowl, combine the spinach, scallions, cherry tomatoes, and mushrooms.

Place the spinach mixture on individual chilled plates and top with the cooked chicken. Sprinkle the blue cheese and almonds on top, and dress with the vinaigrette.

HOW TO TOAST ALMONDS

- Heat a skillet over medium-high heat and add 1 cup of slivered almonds.

- Stir constantly until the almonds are lightly browned.

- Remove from the heat and cool.

Strawberry Spinach Salad

*Try using different nuts and cheeses. Toasted walnuts, pistachios
or macadamia nuts would be good choices. A smoked provolone
or feta cheese could be used instead of the Parmesan.*

6 cups spinach, cleaned and torn into bite-size pieces
¼ cup chopped red onion
½ red pepper, chopped
½ ripe avocado, diced
½ cup sliced strawberries
2-3 tablespoons toasted slivered almonds
Grated Parmesan cheese
Balsamic vinaigrette (page 42)

**In a large serving bowl, combine the spinach, red onion, red pepper, avocado
and strawberries.**

Pour the vinaigrette on the salad and toss.

Sprinkle the Parmesan and top with almonds.

Taco Salad*

Serve with tortilla chips or corn bread.

1 pound lean ground turkey
1/2 onion, finely chopped
1/2 teaspoon salt
Fresh ground pepper
2 cloves garlic, minced
1 4-ounce can diced green chiles
1 14.5-ounce can diced tomatoes with basil, undrained
4 cups romaine lettuce, cleaned and cut into bite-size pieces
1 large tomato, chopped
1/4 cup green onions, sliced
1/3 cup sliced black olives
1 avocado, cut into slices
1 cup grated cheddar cheese

Heat a large frying pan over medium-high heat.

Cook the ground turkey, onion, salt and pepper until no pink remains.

Add the minced garlic and cook for 1 minute.

Drain the browned turkey in a colander and return it to the frying pan.

Add the green chiles and tomatoes to the meat.

Cook over low heat, uncovered, for 30 minutes.

Arrange the lettuce on the bottom of a large chilled bowl.

Pour the cooked meat over this and top with the tomato, green onions, black olives, avocado and cheese.

* *Recipe adapted from* Colorado Cache Cookbook.

Vinaigrette

—MAKES 1/2 CUP—

Vinaigrette is a mixture of oil and vinegar, and is often flavored with herbs, spices and other ingredients.

BASIC VINAIGRETTE

1 small shallot, finely chopped
1 tablespoon Dijon mustard
2 tablespoons balsamic or red wine
   vinegar
6 tablespoons extra virgin olive oil
Salt and fresh ground pepper, to taste

In a small bowl, whisk together the shallot, mustard and vinegar.

Slowly stir in the olive oil.

Add salt and pepper to taste.

RASPBERRY VINAIGRETTE

3 tablespoons raspberry vinegar
1 teaspoon stone ground mustard
1/2-1 teaspoon honey
6 tablespoons walnut oil
Salt and fresh ground pepper, to taste

In a small bowl, whisk together the vinegar, mustard and honey.

Slowly stir in the walnut oil.

Add salt and pepper to taste.

LEMON VINAIGRETTE

2 tablespoons fresh lemon juice
1/2 teaspoon lemon zest
1 teaspoon Dijon mustard
1/4 cup extra virgin olive oil
Salt and fresh ground pepper, to taste

In a small bowl, whisk together the lemon juice, zest and Dijon mustard.

Slowly stir in the olive oil.

Add salt and pepper to taste.

BALSAMIC VINAIGRETTE

1 small shallot, chopped fine
2 tablespoons balsamic vinegar
6 tablespoons olive oil
1 teaspoon honey

In a small bowl, combine the shallots, vinegar, olive oil and honey.

Mix well and set aside.

Soups

There is nothing better to eat on a cold night than a warm bowl of soup. My recipes range from a comforting Tomato Basil to a Hearty Seafood Stew.

Chicken Noodle Soup

—MAKES 8 SERVINGS—

This traditional favorite is a great addition to your soup recipes.
It can stand on its own or be served with a sandwich or salad.

1 whole chicken, cleaned
1 carrot, cleaned and cut into 1-inch
   chunks
1 stalk celery with leaves, cut into
   1-inch chunks
1 medium onion, peeled and
   cut into quarters
2 garlic cloves, peeled
1 teaspoon salt
Fresh ground black pepper, to taste
1 cup finely chopped celery
2 cups carrots, cut into 1/4-inch rounds
2-3 teaspoons chicken base
   (Better than Bouillon™)
1/2 pound cavatelli noodles
1 10-ounce package chopped,
   frozen spinach
Grated Parmesan cheese

In a large soup pan, add the chicken, carrot, celery, onion, garlic, salt and pepper. Cover with cold water and place it over high heat. Heat to where it almost starts to boil, then reduce heat to low. Partially cover with a lid and simmer 1 1/2 hours.

Remove the chicken and cool in the refrigerator.

Strain the broth.

Remove the meat from the bones and refrigerate.

Refrigerate the strained broth overnight.

Remove the fat that hardens on the top and discard.

Place the broth over high heat and bring almost to a boil.

Add the chopped celery, carrots and chicken base. Simmer for 20 minutes.

Bring soup back to a boil and add the noodles. Cook until the noodles are almost done.

Add the frozen spinach and cook for 1 more minute.

Taste the broth and season as needed.

Add the cut-up chicken.

Serve with grated Parmesan cheese.

HOW TO STRAIN BROTH

- While it is still warm, pour the broth through a large fine strainer into a large saucepan. Discard the bones and vegetables.

Chicken Stock

I save and freeze all my carcasses and bones when I roast a chicken. When I want to make a soup, it's nice to have homemade stock in the freezer.

1-2 chicken carcasses

1 teaspoon salt

1 carrot, cut into 2-inch pieces

1 onion, peeled and cut into large
  pieces

2 celery stalks with leaves, cut into
  2-inch pieces

1 leek, washed and cut into large
  pieces

2 stems thyme

1 bay leaf

3 parsley sprigs

2 unpeeled garlic cloves

5 peppercorns

Place bones into a large stockpot and add enough cold water to cover by 1 inch.

Heat over high heat, but do not boil.

Reduce heat to simmer and add the rest of the ingredients.

Skim off the foam from the top as needed. Never allow the liquid to boil.

Simmer the bones for 8 hours, uncovered. Cooking may be stopped at any time and continued later.

Remove from the heat and let cool.

Strain the stock into a large bowl. Discard the bones and vegetables.

Refrigerate the stock overnight. Remove the fat from the top of the stock and discard.

Reheat the stock and season to taste. Let broth boil gently for 20-30 minutes.

Stock can be frozen and used later.

Minestrone Soup

—MAKES 8 SERVINGS—

This makes a large amount and freezes well. It's a good way to use leftover meat.

1 tablespoon olive oil
1 large onion, chopped
1 stalk celery with leaves, chopped
½ teaspoon salt
Fresh ground black pepper, to taste
2 cloves garlic, minced
1 28-ounce can diced tomatoes
4 cups vegetable, chicken or beef broth
2 tablespoons chopped fresh parsley,
   or 1 teaspoon dried
1 ½ teaspoons dried basil
½ teaspoon dried oregano
1 bay leaf
½ cup brown rice
1 15-ounce can red kidney beans,
   rinsed and drained
2 carrots, sliced
2 cups leftover meat
   (chicken, steak, ham)
1 small package frozen,
   chopped spinach
Grated Romano or Parmesan cheese

Heat a large soup pan over medium-high heat.

Add the oil, onion, celery, salt and pepper. Sauté for 10 minutes.

Add the minced garlic and cook for 1 minute.

Add the tomatoes, broth, parsley, basil, oregano and bay leaf.

Bring to a boil, partially cover, and simmer for 20 minutes.

Add the brown rice, cover and simmer for 25 minutes.

Add the kidney beans and carrots. Simmer for 15 minutes.

Add the frozen spinach and meat; stir and simmer for 5 minutes.

Remove the bay leaf.

Garnish with cheese.

Pumpkin Soup

—MAKES 8 SERVINGS—

This soup can also be made using cooked squash, yams or sweet potatoes. The recipe was adapted from The Duck Soup Restaurant in San Juan Island, Washington.

1 tablespoon canola oil

1 onion, diced

1 stalk celery with leaves, diced

1 tablespoon fresh ginger, chopped fine

1 carrot, sliced

1/2 teaspoon salt

Fresh ground black pepper

2 cups white wine (chardonnay or pinot grigio)

10 cups chicken stock

4 cups pumpkin purée (fresh or canned)

1/4 teaspoon cinnamon

1/4 teaspoon ground cloves

1 piece star anise

1 tablespoon lime juice

1 teaspoon rice wine vinegar

1/8 teaspoon cayenne pepper

HOW TO DEGLAZE

- After you finish the sauté, remove the excess fat. You will notice small amounts of flavor-rich browned food particles stuck to the sauté pan.

- To loosen these bits, just add a small amount of liquid (wine, stock or lemon juice, for example) to the pan and start stirring.

- It is important to remove the pan from the heat when adding any liquids containing alcohol.

Heat a large soup pan over medium-high heat.

Add the oil, onion, celery, ginger, carrot, salt and pepper. Sauté for 5 minutes.

Add the white wine and deglaze over medium-high heat. (Reduce the liquid until it is almost dry.)

Add the chicken stock, pumpkin purée and spices.

Bring to boil, reduce heat and simmer for 45 minutes.

Season with the lime juice and rice wine vinegar.

Stir in the cayenne pepper. Salt and pepper to taste.

Seafood Stew

—MAKES 8 SERVINGS—

Fennel is a popular herb in Italy. It can be thinly sliced and eaten plain, or used as part of a vegetable platter. It can also be chopped up into salad similar to celery.

2 tablespoons olive oil
1 fennel bulb, chopped
1 onion, chopped
2 large shallots, chopped
1 ½ teaspoons salt
Fresh ground pepper
6 cloves garlic, minced
½–1 teaspoon red pepper flakes
1 teaspoon dried oregano
½ teaspoon dried basil
4 tablespoons tomato paste
1 28-ounce can crushed tomatoes
1 ½ cups dry white or red wine
1 cup bottled clam juice
5 cups chicken broth
1 bay leaf
1 pound Manila clams, scrubbed
1 pound mussels, scrubbed and
  debearded
1 pound uncooked large shrimp,
  peeled and deveined
¾ pound sea scallops, tough muscle
  removed from side of each, if
  necessary
1 pound skinless salmon, cut into bite-size pieces
1 pound halibut, cut into bite-size pieces
¼ cup finely chopped fresh flat-leaf parsley
¼ cup finely chopped fresh basil

HOW TO PREPARE FENNEL

- Cut the stalks off the bulb.
- Remove any discolored or tough outer leaves and trim the base of the bulb.
- If slicing the bulb vertically, the inner core will hold the leaves together.
- To slice slivers or quarters, cut out the dense core and discard it.
- Save the stalks for soups, stews or braising.
- The leaves can be used the same way as fresh dill or as a garnish.

Seafood Stew (continued)

Heat a large soup pan over medium-high heat. Add oil, fennel, onion, shallot, salt and pepper. Sauté for 10 minutes.

Add the garlic, red pepper, oregano, basil, and tomato paste. Stir until blended. Add the crushed tomatoes, wine, clam juice, chicken broth and bay leaf. Partially cover and simmer for 30 minutes.

Add the clams and mussels. Cover and cook until they begin to open — about 5 minutes.

Lightly season the shrimp, scallops and salmon with salt. Add to the stew and simmer, covered, until cooked — about 5 minutes.

Discard any clams or mussels that did not open. Discard bay leaf.

Season to taste. Garnish with the parsley and basil.

Tomato Basil Soup

—MAKES 8 SERVINGS—

Chickpeas are also known as garbanzo beans.
They are used to thicken this soup and add fiber.

2 tablespoons olive oil
1 onion, finely chopped
2-3 carrots, peeled and finely chopped
2 stalks celery with leaves, finely chopped
½ teaspoon salt
Fresh ground black pepper
2 cloves garlic, finely chopped
2 28-ounce cans diced tomatoes
4 tablespoons tomato paste
3 cups chicken broth
¼ cup finely chopped fresh basil
1 can chickpeas, rinsed and drained
½ teaspoon sugar
1 cup fat-free milk or fat-free half and half
Grated Parmesan cheese

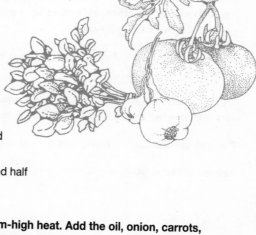

Heat a large soup pot over medium-high heat. Add the oil, onion, carrots, celery, salt and pepper. Sauté for 10 minutes.

Add the garlic and cook for 1 minute.

Add the tomatoes, tomato paste, chicken broth, basil, chickpeas and sugar.

Bring to a boil, reduce to a simmer and cook, partially covered, for 30 minutes.

Using a blender, purée the soup in small batches, and return it to the saucepan.

Heat the soup over medium-high heat.

Add the milk, stirring occasionally, until the soup is the desired temperature.

Season to taste.

Serve in soup bowls topped with grated Parmesan cheese.

Slow Cooker

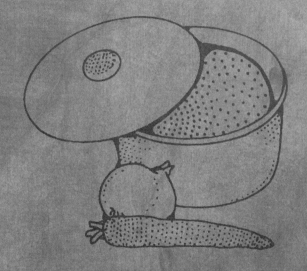

My slow cooker gets a lot of use, especially during the week. I can fix our dinner in the morning or even the night before.

Chicken with Celery Root and Garlic

—MAKES 6 SERVINGS—

Celery root has a pungent celery-like flavor and is a variety of celery. In recipes calling for cauliflower or fennel, celery root makes an interesting substitute.

2 to 3 pounds chicken parts (legs, thighs or breasts), skin and fat removed
Salt and pepper, to taste
1 teaspoon canola oil
1 teaspoon butter
1 celery root, cut into ¾-inch pieces, or base of a head of celery
2 tablespoons chopped celery leaves
6 cloves garlic, peeled

¼ cup dry white wine
1 ¼ cups chicken broth
2 sprigs fresh thyme, or ¼ teaspoon dried
4 red potatoes, cut into 1½-inch chunks
2 tablespoons chopped flat-leaf parsley
Sour cream

Sprinkle the chicken pieces with salt and pepper. Place into the slow cooker.

Heat a frying pan over medium-high heat. Add the oil and butter, celery root and celery leaves. Sauté for 4 minutes or until slightly browned.

Add the garlic cloves and continue to cook for 1 minute.

Carefully pour in the wine and reduce the liquid for 2 minutes.  Add this to the slow cooker.

Pour the chicken broth over the chicken and add the thyme and potatoes.

On high, cover and cook for 1 hour.

Reduce to low and continue to cook for 6-8 hours.

Serve in a large bowl with the parsley sprinkled on top. The sour cream makes a great topping for the potatoes.

HOW TO REDUCE LIQUID

- Simmer or boil a liquid so that some of the water evaporates.
- This concentrates the liquid so it has more flavor.

Southwest Chicken Chili

I used leftover turkey in this after Thanksgiving and it was wonderful.

2 teaspoons canola oil
1 medium yellow onion, chopped
½ cup chopped celery
Salt and pepper, to taste
2 cloves garlic, minced
1 teaspoon ground cumin
1 15.5-ounce can small white beans, rinsed and drained
1 15.5-ounce can garbanzo beans, rinsed and drained
1 cup white corn, canned, fresh or frozen
1 2.4-ounce can mild chopped green chiles
1 ½ cups fat-free chicken broth
4 cups cooked chicken or turkey, cut into bite-size pieces
1 cup grated Monterey jack or cheddar cheese

Heat a large frying pan over medium-high heat. Add the oil, onion, celery, salt and pepper. Cook for 5 minutes.

Add the garlic and cook for 1 minute.

Pour these into a slow cooker and add the cumin, beans, corn, chiles, chicken broth and chicken. Stir until blended.

Place lid on the slow cooker and turn on high for 1 hour.

Reduce to low and cook for 6-7 hours.

Serve with grated cheese sprinkled on top of each bowl of chili.

Irish Lamb Stew

One of the great things about Irish cooking is that the raw ingredients are just about the best anywhere. You probably haven't had lamb until you've had lamb from Ireland, so find the best quality you can for this dish. It's hearty, filling and great for a cold night.

1 tablespoon canola oil

1 ½ pounds lamb, cut into 2-inch cubes

Salt and pepper, to taste

1 clove garlic, minced

2 cups white wine or chicken broth

2 cups beef broth

½ pound frozen pearl onions

2 sweet potatoes, cut into 2-inch pieces

2 Yukon Gold potatoes, cut into 2-inch pieces

1 10-ounce package frozen peas, thawed

2 tablespoons chopped fresh parsley

2 sprigs thyme, or ½ teaspoon dried

1 teaspoon chopped fresh rosemary or ½ teaspoon dried

½ teaspoon salt

Fresh ground pepper to taste

4 tablespoons spelt flour

½ cup cold water

Mint sauce or jelly

Heat a large frying pan over medium-high heat. Add oil.

Salt and pepper the lamb and put it in the pan.

Brown the lamb on all sides and place it in the slow cooker.

Add the minced garlic, wine, broth, onions, potatoes, peas, parsley, thyme, rosemary, salt and pepper.

Cover and cook on high for 1 hour.

Turn down to low and cook for 6 hours.

In a small bowl, combine the flour and cold water until blended.

Add to the slow cooker and stir.

Turn slow cooker back to high and cook for 30 minutes or until thickened.

Serve with mint sauce or jelly for the lamb.

Pork Roast with Sauerkraut

—MAKES 4 SERVINGS—

This recipe was given to my by my friend Deanne Demarco.
I like to serve it with applesauce and a green salad.

2 teaspoons canola oil
2 pounds pork roast
Salt and pepper, to taste
½ cup dry white wine
1 32-ounce jar sauerkraut, undrained

Heat a heavy frying pan over medium-high heat. Add the oil and the pork roast.

Brown on all sides, seasoning with salt and pepper as you turn.

Remove the pork from the pan and place it into the slow cooker.

Add the wine to the frying pan and cook over medium-high heat for 1-2 minutes, scraping the bottom of the pan. Place the pan drippings into the slow cooker.

Pour the undrained sauerkraut over the pork and cook on high heat, covered, for 1 hour.

Reduce to low and continue to cook until the pork is tender — 6-8 hours.

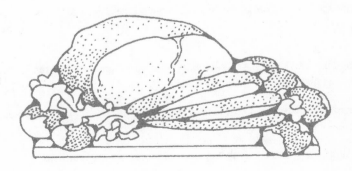

Pot Roast and Gravy

—MAKES 4 SERVINGS—

Pot Roast is a method of slowly cooking meat in a covered pot. It produces moist meat, making it ideal for less-expensive cuts of meat.

2 tablespoons canola oil
2 pounds beef chuck roast
Salt and pepper, to taste
1 packet onion soup mix
3 cups water
4 Yukon Gold potatoes, cut into 2-inch pieces
4 carrots, cut into 1-inch pieces
1 yellow onion, cut into 1-inch pieces

Heat a large frying pan over medium-high heat.

Salt and pepper the chuck roast and add to the pan.

Cook until the meat is brown on both sides, about 5 minutes.

Place the browned chuck roast into a slow cooker. Add the onion soup mix, water, potatoes, carrots and onion.

Cover and cook on high for 1 hour.

Turn down to low and cook for 6-7 hours or until meat falls apart.

Remove meat, potatoes and carrots and place on a warm serving dish.
You can make gravy out of the broth or save it for soup later.

GRAVY

In a medium bowl, place 4 tablespoons flour and ½ cup cold water. Shake or whisk until blended.

In a medium saucepan, heat the beef broth over high heat and slowly add the flour mixture.

Reduce the heat and stir until thickened. Simmer for 2-3 minutes.

Season to taste.

Entrées

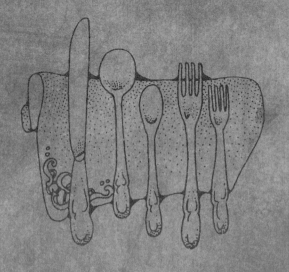

1. "The course following the fish course in a French classic menu. Generally well garnished and served with a gravy or sauce." — Web definition

2. "The main course of a meal in the United States."
—*Merriam-Webster's dictionary*

Chicken with Fresh Mozzarella and Noodles

This is a recipe my son Daniel shared with me. I've used leftover chicken and it's great with some chopped kalamata olives and capers added.

4 skinless and boneless chicken breasts, or 6-8 chicken tenders
Salt and pepper, to taste
2 tablespoons olive oil
1 pound penne pasta
3 cups marinara sauce
¼ cup fresh basil, cut into thin strips
1 pound fresh mozzarella roll, sliced into ¼-inch rounds
¼ cup grated Parmesan cheese

Preheat oven to 350°F.

Place the chicken in a 9x11 casserole dish that has been sprayed with nonstick cooking spray.

**Salt and pepper the chicken breast and drizzle the olive oil over the top.
Bake for 25-35 minutes or until almost done. It should be slightly pink inside.**

Remove chicken from the oven and cut into bite-size pieces.

Cook the pasta until almost done. It should still have a slight bite to it. Drain.

Layer half of the pasta on the bottom of a large oiled casserole dish. Pour half of the marinara sauce over the pasta. Place half of the cut-up chicken on the sauce and top with half of the fresh basil. Place half of the mozzarella on the basil. Sprinkle on half of the Parmesan cheese.

Repeat the layers and cover with aluminum foil.

Bake for 30 minutes or until heated through.

Chili

My sister Janet gave me this recipe and it is now my favorite.
Serve with corn bread and a green salad.

4 teaspoons canola oil

2 onions, chopped

1 pound lean ground turkey

Salt and pepper, to taste

3 chopped carrots

3 chopped celery stalks with leaves

2 cloves garlic, minced

1 28-ounce can diced tomatoes

1 15-ounce can tomato sauce

2 tablespoons tomato paste

2 15-ounce cans white beans, drained
and rinsed

1 28-ounce can red kidney beans,
drained and rinsed

2 tablespoons chili powder

⅛ teaspoon chipotle powder

2-3 tablespoons mild chili flakes

1 tablespoon medium chili flakes

Heat 2 teaspoons of the oil in a 5-quart saucepan. Add half of the chopped onion, turkey, salt and pepper. Cook until done.

Drain off the excess liquid.

Heat a medium sauté pan over medium-high heat. Add the remaining 2 teaspoons of oil. Add the carrots, celery and the rest of the chopped onion. Sauté until soft.

Add the minced garlic and cook for 1 minute. Add this to the meat mixture.

Place the diced tomatoes, tomato sauce, tomato paste, beans, chili powder, chipotle and chili flakes into the saucepan and bring to a boil.

Simmer for 1 hour.

Cracker~Crumb Pork Chops

—MAKES 4 SERVINGS—

Breading and baking the pork chops makes them very tender.
I always like to serve applesauce with pork.

2 egg whites, slightly beaten
1 teaspoon water
½ teaspoon seasoning salt
4 pork chops, bone-in
1 cup crushed soda crackers, low-sodium or wheat

Preheat oven to 325°F.

Mix together the egg whites, water and salt. Pour on a plate.

Place the crushed crackers on another plate.

Dip the pork chop into the egg mixture and then roll in the cracker crumbs.

Spray a casserole dish with nonstick spray.

Place the chops in the dish. Bake for 1 ½ hours.

Enchiladas

This is an easy dish. It is tasty and a great way to use leftover meat.

2 teaspoons canola oil
½ cup onion, finely chopped
1 clove garlic, minced
1 15-ounce can chopped tomatoes with basil
1 4-ounce can diced green chiles
½ teaspoon cumin
¼ teaspoon oregano
½ teaspoon dried basil
Salt and pepper, to taste
2 cups shredded cooked pork or chicken
1 ½ cups shredded Monterey jack or cheddar cheese
6 whole-grain tortillas

Preheat oven to 350°F.

Heat a medium frying pan over medium-high heat. Add the oil and onion, and cook for 5 minutes.

Add the minced garlic and cook for 1 minute.

Add the tomatoes, green chiles, cumin, oregano, basil, salt and pepper. Stir in the chicken.

Bring to a boil, reduce heat, cover and simmer for 15 minutes.

Place 4 tablespoons of the chicken mixture and 2 tablespoons of the cheese on each tortilla.

Roll up and place seam-side down in a greased 9x11 pan.

Brush the remaining tomato liquid on the top of the tortillas so they don't dry out.

Sprinkle the top with the remaining cheese.

Cover with aluminum foil and bake for 40 minutes.

Roast Chicken with Garlic

—MAKES 6 SERVINGS—

Turn the chicken every 15 minutes in the oven while roasting.
This creates even browning.

1 5-pound roasting chicken
1 tablespoon olive oil
3 cloves garlic, minced
1 teaspoon lemon zest
2 teaspoons thyme
Salt and pepper, to taste
1 lemon, quartered

Preheat oven to 425°F.

Mix the olive oil, garlic, lemon zest and thyme in a small bowl.

Clean the chicken and pat dry with a paper towel.

Salt and pepper the inside of the bird and place the quartered lemon inside the cavity. Rub the olive oil mixture over the inside and outside of the bird.

Roast, uncovered, for 90 minutes or until done. Bird is done when then the inside thigh temperature reaches 170°F.

Let the bird sit for 10 minutes before carving.

Roast Chicken with Citrus

1 5-pound roasting chicken
1 citrus fruit, quartered, (orange, lemon or grapefruit)
1 tablespoon olive oil
Salt and pepper, to taste

Preheat oven to 425°F.

Clean the chicken and pat dry with a paper towel.

Rub the olive oil over the bird and salt and pepper the inside of the bird. Place the citrus inside the cavity.

Bake, uncovered, for 90 minutes or until done. The chicken is done when the inside thigh temperature reaches 170°F.

Let the bird sit for 10 minutes before carving.

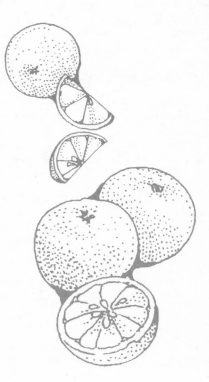

HOW TO USE A MEAT THERMOMETER

- Place the meat thermometer in center of inside thigh muscle not touching the bone.

- There are three ways to check if the bird is done:

  1) Thermometer reaches 170°F.
  2) The juices inside the bird run clear.
  3) The legs easily pull away from the bird.

Hamburgers – Mary's Style

—MAKES 4 SERVINGS—

These burgers are so moist and tasty. I like to top them with caramelized onions and an assortment of mustards.

1 pound lean ground turkey
½ onion, grated
1 tablespoon coarse-grain mustard
½ teaspoon dried basil
½ teaspoon dried oregano
½ teaspoon dried thyme
½ teaspoon ground cumin
Cracked black pepper, to taste
⅛ teaspoon salt

**In a large bowl, combine
all ingredients.**

Mix by hand until blended.

Form into 4-5 patties.

Grill or broil.

Paprika Chicken and Gravy

—MAKES 6 SERVINGS—

Paprika is a red powder made from grinding dried sweet red peppers and is used as a garnish and seasoning. The color varies from bright orange-red to deep red, depending on the peppers used. Most commercial paprika comes from Spain, South America, California and Hungary. Hungarian paprika is thought to be the finest (Kitchen Dictionary).

2 teaspoons canola oil
1 medium onion, finely chopped
Salt and pepper, to taste
1 tablespoon sweet Hungarian paprika
1 chicken, cut into 8 pieces, skinned if desired
1 15.5-ounce can chopped tomatoes
1/2 red pepper, finely diced
1/4 cup chicken broth
1/4 cup light sour cream
1 1/2 teaspoons flour

Heat a large frying pan over medium-high heat. Add the oil, onion, salt and pepper.

Sauté for 10 minutes.

Add the paprika and cook for 1 minute.

Add the chicken pieces, tomatoes, red pepper and chicken broth. Bring to a boil.

Reduce heat to low, cover with a lid and cook for 1 hour or until done.

Remove the chicken to a warm plate and cover with aluminum foil to keep it warm.

Bring the juices in the pan to a boil and cook until they reduce to 1 cup.

Pour 1/2 cup of the hot pan juice in a small bowl. Add the sour cream and flour.

Stir, add it back to the pan and combine well.

Heat and serve over the chicken.

Italian Meatballs

These are healthier because you cook them in the oven.
Make a batch and freeze the other half for later.

1 ½ pounds lean ground turkey or ½ pound each ground beef, veal and pork
½ cup grated onion
2 cloves garlic, minced
1 egg, slightly beaten
2 tablespoons chopped fresh flat-leaf parsley
½ cup old-fashioned oats
½ cup Parmesan cheese
¼ teaspoon salt
Fresh ground pepper

Preheat the oven to 350°F.

Place all the ingredients into a large bowl. Gently mix with your hands until blended.

With wet hands, form the meat mixture into 1 ½-inch balls.

Place them on a broiler pan that has been sprayed with nonstick spray and bake for 20 minutes.

Place them in marinara sauce (page 69) and simmer for 30 minutes or until done.

Joe's Special

—MAKES 4 SERVINGS—

I first had this dish 35 years ago in a little Italian restaurant in Bellevue, Washington. I loved it then and still enjoy all the great flavors. Serve with whole-grain bread and a green salad.

1 pound Italian chicken sausage
1 pound lean ground turkey
2 teaspoons canola oil
1 Walla Walla or Spanish onion, chopped
Salt and pepper, to taste
1/2 pound crimini mushrooms, sliced
3 small green or yellow zucchini, cut
  lengthwise and into 1/2-inch half rounds
3 cloves garlic, minced
1 pound frozen chopped spinach, thawed
  and squeezed to remove liquid
1 egg and 2 egg whites, slightly beaten
1/4 cup grated Parmesan cheese

Heat a large frying pan over medium-high heat. Add the sausage and turkey and cook until done.

Drain the meat in a colander and set aside.

Add the canola oil to the same pan and heat over medium-high heat. Add the onion, salt and pepper and cook for 5 minutes.

Add the mushrooms and cook for 5 more minutes.

Add the zucchini and cook for 3 minutes.

Add the garlic and cook for 1 minute.

Fold in the drained spinach, meat and eggs. Cook for 2 minutes or until eggs are cooked.

Serve in a large bowl and top with Parmesan cheese.

Lamb Shish Kebab

Shish kebab started as a Turkish dish of skewered, marinated lamb.
Today, I cube and skewer just about anything.
Everything tastes better on a stick.

1 teaspoon fresh rosemary, or ½ teaspoon dried
1 tablespoon fresh mint leaves
2 cloves garlic, pressed
½ teaspoon kosher salt
Fresh ground pepper, to taste
2 tablespoons canola oil
1 tablespoon red wine vinegar
1 ¼ pounds lean lamb steaks cut into 1-inch cubes
¼ red onion, cut into 2-inch chunks

Finely chop the rosemary and mint.

To prepare the marinade, combine the garlic, salt, pepper, rosemary and mint in a small bowl. Add the oil and vinegar.

Place the cut-up lamb into a ziploc bag. Add the marinade and seal the bag. Refrigerate for 4 hours.

Thread the lamb and red onion onto skewers and grill until done. These can be cooked on a barbecue or broiled in the oven.

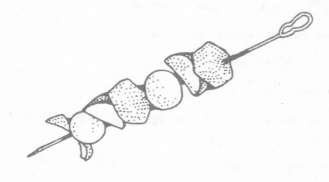

Marinara Sauce

*This is a good red sauce base. You can add capers, kalamata olives,
spinach, meatballs, cooked Italian sausage or prawns. The list is endless.
Serve over your favorite pasta with a salad and crusty bread.*

2 teaspoons olive oil
½ cup chopped onion
4 cloves garlic, minced
1 28-ounce can chopped tomatoes
⅓ cup red wine, such as zinfandel
½ cup fresh basil, minced
1 tablespoon dried oregano
½ teaspoon salt
Fresh ground black pepper, to taste
1 6-ounce can tomato paste

**Heat a large frying pan over medium-high heat. Add the oil and onion and cook
for 5 minutes.**

Add the minced garlic and cook for 1 minute more.

**Slowly add the chopped tomatoes, wine, fresh basil, oregano, salt and pepper.
Bring to a slow boil, reduce heat and simmer for 15 minutes.**

Add the tomato paste and simmer for an additional 15 minutes.

VARIATION

**Try adding 3 tablespoons rinsed capers, 2 cups fresh
spinach leaves and 1 pound large prawns.**

Cook in sauce until prawns are done, about 3-5 minutes.

Marinated Flank Steak

—MAKES 4 SERVINGS—

I like to keep a few marinated flank steaks in the freezer. When I have unexpected company, I pull one out and start dinner.

1 ½ pounds beef flank steak
2 tablespoons coarse ground mustard
2 tablespoons low-sodium soy sauce
2 tablespoons lime juice
2-3 cloves garlic, minced
½ teaspoon dried ginger, or 1 teaspoon chopped fresh ginger
2 teaspoons hoisin sauce*
½ teaspoon Worcestershire sauce

In a small bowl, mix the mustard, soy sauce, lime juice, garlic, ginger, Hoisin and Worcestershire sauce.

Place the flank steak in a large ziploc bag and pour the marinade over the steak.

Marinade for 3 to 24 hours or freeze.

Grill for 4 to 6 minutes on each side for a medium-rare steak. Cook each side for 1 to 2 minutes more for a medium-well steak.

Remove the steak from the heat and let it stand for 5 minutes.

Thinly slice the steak across the grain.

* Hoisin sauce can be found in the Asian section of your grocery store.

One~Pot Italian Sausage and Potatoes

—MAKES 4 SERVINGS—

Italian chicken sausage is low in fat and adds a lot of flavor to this one-pot dish. An 8-inch cast-iron skillet works great, but any ovenproof frying pan will do.

2 teaspoons canola oil
1 pound Italian chicken sausage
1/2 pound sweet potatoes, peeled and cut into 1/4-inch slices
1/2 pound red potatoes, peeled and cut into 1/4-inch slices
Salt and pepper, to taste
1 10.8-ounce bag frozen chopped spinach, cooked and drained of all liquid
Pinch dried nutmeg
2 cups fresh tomatoes, seeded and chopped
1/2 teaspoon dried oregano
2 tablespoons fresh basil, torn into small pieces, or 1/2 teaspoon dried

Preheat oven to 350°F.

In a cast-iron frying pan over medium-high heat, add the oil and sausage and cook until done.

Remove the sausage from the pan and drain in a colander.

Remove the pan from the heat and wipe it out with a paper towel. Spray with nonstick cooking spray.

Place the meat back into the pan, spreading it around evenly.

Layer the sliced sweet and red potatoes over the meat. Salt and pepper to taste. Place the spinach on top of the potatoes and sprinkle the nutmeg over the spinach. Add the tomatoes, oregano and basil.

Cover with aluminum foil and bake for 1 hour.

Pork Tenderloin

1 ½ pounds pork tenderloin
1 tablespoon yellow curry paste
1 tablespoon olive oil
Salt and pepper, to taste

Place the pork tenderloin on a piece of plastic wrap. Rub the olive oil and curry paste over the pork with your hands.

Wrap meat up in the plastic and marinate for 1 hour.

Barbeque for 12 minutes on both sides over 400°F heat or until internal temperature reaches 155°F.

Remove from heat and let sit for 10 minutes.

Slice on the diagonal.

Quiche

—MAKES 6 SERVINGS—

This quiche is so easy to make. Use leftover vegetables or meats to create a wonderful dish. Serve with a green salad and fruit.

1 9-inch single pie crust
4 eggs
1 ½ cups grated Swiss cheese
⅓ cup grated Parmesan cheese
1 ½ cups nonfat milk or nonfat half-and-half
⅛ teaspoon salt
Fresh ground pepper
1 tablespoon chopped fresh parsley
Any of the following additional ingredients:
  Crumpled bacon, sautéed mushrooms and onion, black olives, leftover asparagus or broccoli, ham, cooked Italian sausage, etc.

Preheat oven to 350°F.

Mix the egg, cheeses, milk, salt and pepper in a blender.

Pour into a large bowl and stir in the extra ingredients.

Pour this into the crust.

Bake for 1 hour or until done. It is done when a knife placed in the center comes out clean.

Let sit for 10 minutes.

Garnish with Italian parsley.

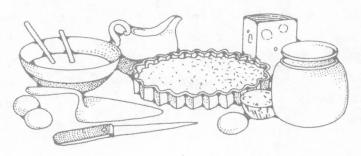

Roast Turkey

—MAKES 12 SERVINGS—

This is an easy way to cook a turkey. Enjoy it at Thanksgiving or any night of the week. The leftovers are great.

One 18-pound turkey, defrosted
Olive oil
Sea salt
1 carrot, scrubbed and cut in half
1 stalk celery with leaves, cut in half
1 yellow onion, peeled and cut into
   quarters

Preheat oven to 325°F. Position the rack as low as possible in the oven.

Remove the neck and giblets from the turkey cavities. Rinse the turkey well on both the outside and inside. Pat dry. Tie the drumsticks together with kitchen string. Rub the outside of the bird with olive oil and salt the inside of the bird.

Place the carrot, celery and onion in the bottom of a large roasting pan. Place the turkey, breast side up, on top of the vegetables. Insert a meat thermometer into the center of one of the inside thigh muscles. The bulb should not touch the bone.

Place the bird in the oven and baste every 30 minutes with the pan juices after the first hour. Turkey is done when the thermometer reads 180°.

Remove turkey from the oven, cover with aluminum foil and let it sit for 30 minutes before carving.

TURKEY ROASTING TIMES

Unstuffed Turkey		Stuffed Turkey	
8 to 12 lbs:	2 $\frac{3}{4}$ to 3 hours	8 to 12 lbs:	3 to 3 $\frac{1}{2}$ hours
12 to 14 lbs:	3 to 3 $\frac{3}{4}$ hours	12 to 14 lbs:	3 $\frac{1}{2}$ to 4 hours
14 to 18 lbs:	3 $\frac{3}{4}$ to 4 $\frac{1}{4}$ hours	14 to 18 lbs:	4 to 4 $\frac{1}{4}$ hours
18 to 20 lbs:	4 $\frac{1}{4}$ to 4 $\frac{1}{2}$ hours	18 to 20 lbs:	4 $\frac{1}{4}$ to 4 $\frac{3}{4}$ hours
20 to 24 lbs:	4 $\frac{1}{2}$ to 5 hours	20 to 24 lbs:	4 $\frac{3}{4}$ to 5 $\frac{1}{4}$ hours

Dressing for Roast Turkey

—MAKES 12 SERVINGS—

2 teaspoon olive oil

1 shallot, finely chopped

½ cup celery, finely chopped

½ cup carrot, finely chopped

Salt and pepper, to taste

1 package stuffing mix with herbs

1 15-ounce can reduced-fat chicken broth

1 10.75-ounce can Healthy Request® Cream of Mushroom soup

1 tablespoon chopped parsley

Heat a large frying pan over medium-high heat. Add the oil, shallot, celery, carrot, salt and pepper. Cook for 5 minutes.

Add the stuffing mix with herbs, chicken broth and mushroom soup. Stir until blended.

Fold in the parsley. Place in a greased casserole dish, cover and bake at 325° for 50 minutes.

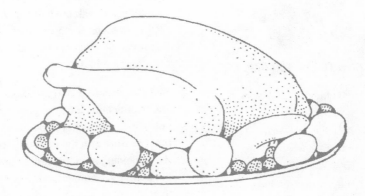

Stuffed Red Peppers

—MAKES 4 SERVINGS—

Sweet red peppers are actually green peppers left to ripen on the vine for a longer period of time. The sweetest peppers are red, yellow and orange. Try using different colored peppers.

2 large red peppers

2 teaspoons canola oil

½ yellow onion, finely chopped

Salt and pepper, to taste

1 celery stalk with leaves, finely chopped

1 pound Italian chicken sausage

1 large clove garlic, minced

1 14.5-ounce can diced tomatoes
   with basil and oregano

1 teaspoon Worcestershire sauce

½ teaspoon dried oregano

1 bay leaf

1 cup cooked brown rice

Salt and pepper

½ cup grated low-fat cheddar cheese

HOW TO BLANCH PEPPERS

- First bring a pot of water to a boil.

- Add the peppers and boil for 3 minutes.

- Remove peppers from the water and place them in a bowl of ice water.

- Let them cool and then drain.

Preheat oven to 375°F.

Rinse the peppers and cut them in half lengthwise. Remove the seeds and white membranes. Blanch for 3 minutes and drain.

Heat a large frying pan over medium-high heat. Add the oil, onion and celery, and season with salt and pepper. Cook for 4 minutes.

Add the sausage and brown until there is no pink remaining.

Add the garlic and cook for 1 minute.

Stir in the tomatoes, Worcestershire sauce, oregano, bay leaf and rice. Season again with the salt and pepper to taste. Bring to a boil. Reduce heat to simmer, cover and cook for 15 minutes.

Spray a casserole dish with non-stick spray and place the peppers cut-side up in the pan. Spoon the meat mixture into the peppers, with the remaining meat placed around the peppers. Sprinkle grated cheese over the tops.

Bake uncovered for 15 minutes or until heated through.

Swedish Meatballs

This dish is great served with brown rice and steamed broccoli.

1 pound lean ground turkey
½ onion, grated
¼ cup old-fashioned oats
1 egg
2 tablespoons fresh chopped parsley
Salt and pepper, to taste

Dash ground nutmeg
Dash ground ginger
1 tablespoon olive oil
1 can Healthy Request®
  Cream of Mushroom soup
½ cup fat-free milk

Preheat the oven to 350°F.

In a large bowl, combine the ground turkey, grated onion, oats, egg, chopped parsley, salt, pepper, nutmeg and ginger. Mix all the ingredients by hand until blended. With damp hands, form the meat mixture into 2-inch balls.

In a nonstick frying pan, heat the olive oil over medium-high heat. Place half of the formed meatballs into the hot oil and cook on one side for 4 minutes.

Turn the meatballs and cook until all sides are browned. Remove them from the pan and brown the remaining meatballs.

Place the browned meatballs into a casserole dish sprayed with nonstick spray.

In a medium bowl, combine the mushroom soup and milk. Stir until blended and pour over the meatballs. Cover with a lid and place in the oven. Cook for 1 hour.

BAKING ALTERNATIVE

Preheat oven to 350°F.

Spray a broiler pan with nonstick spray. Place the meatballs on the pan and cook for 20 minutes.

Remove and place into prepared casserole dish.

Cover with soup and milk, and bake as above.

Chicken Stir Fry with Peanut Sauce

—MAKES 4 SERVINGS—

Serve this delicious dish with brown rice and sliced kiwi.
Adapted from The Mayo Clinic Williams-Sonoma cookbook.

1/4 cup creamy peanut butter

2 tablespoons reduced-sodium soy sauce

2 tablespoons lime juice

1/3 cup water

2 teaspoons sesame oil

2 teaspoons cornstarch

1/4 teaspoon crushed red pepper flakes

2 tablespoons canola oil

1 pound chicken breast, cut into bite-size pieces

12 ounces white button mushrooms, sliced

1 stalk celery, sliced diagonally

2 carrots, sliced thin diagonally

1/2 onion, cut into 2-inch pieces

1 pound snow peas

8 ounces sliced water chestnuts, rinsed and drained

1/2 cup chopped peanuts

In a small bowl, whisk together the peanut butter, soy sauce and lime juice until smooth. Add the water, sesame oil, cornstarch and pepper flakes. Whisk until blended.

Heat a large frying pan over medium-high heat. Add the oil and chicken, and cook until done.

Remove the chicken from the pan and set aside.

Add the mushrooms, celery, carrots and onion to the pan and stir-fry until lightly browned, about 4 minutes.

Add the snow peas and continue stir-frying until the peas are tender, for 2-3 minutes.

Return the chicken to the vegetables and add the peanut butter mixture. Stir until the sauce thickens, about 1 minute.

Fold in the water chestnuts. Top with the chopped peanuts.

Turkey Meatloaf

—MAKES 4 SERVINGS—

This is my favorite dish to serve for dinner. I always have the ingredients on hand and it is so fast and easy to put together. Bake a few sweet potatoes and cook a green vegetable — dinner is served.

1 pound lean ground turkey
½ cup old-fashioned oats
½ medium onion, grated
1 egg, slightly beaten
2 tablespoons ketchup
1 teaspoon Worcestershire sauce
½ teaspoon salt
Fresh ground pepper, to taste

Preheat oven to 350°F.

Spray a casserole dish with nonstick cooking spray.

In a medium bowl, combine all the ingredients. Gently mix with your hands until blended, but do not overmix.

Form this into a loaf and place on the prepared dish.

Bake for 1 hour or until done. Let meatloaf rest 10 minutes before slicing.

Seafood

Eating fresh fish has many advantages. It is high in protein, low in saturated fat and contains high percentages of omega-3 fatty acids.

Baked Lemon Salmon

—MAKES 2 SERVINGS—

I like to cook my salmon with the skin on.
It stays moist and is easy to serve.

1 pound wild salmon
2 tablespoons melted butter
1 teaspoon Worcestershire sauce
2 teaspoons grated onion
1 tablespoon lemon juice
½ teaspoon lemon zest
¼ teaspoon salt
Fresh ground black pepper

Preheat oven to 350°F.

Spray a 9x9-inch ovenproof dish with nonstick cooking spray. Place the salmon, skin side down, in the dish.

In a medium mixing bowl, combine the melted butter, Worcestershire sauce, grated onion, lemon juice, lemon zest and salt and pepper.

Spoon sauces over the salmon and bake for 25-30 minutes or until done. Salmon should flake in the middle.

Grilled Salmon

—MAKES 2 SERVINGS—

The flavor of the honey combined with the vinegar
gives this dish a sweet, tangy taste.

½ cup honey, melted slightly in the microwave
¼ cup balsamic vinegar
1 pound wild salmon
¼ teaspoon Coleman's dry mustard
¼ teaspoon salt
Fresh ground pepper
2 tablespoons melted butter

In a small bowl, combine the honey and vinegar.

Score the salmon and rub the mustard, salt and pepper over the top.

Spoon on the butter.

Place on the barbeque over medium-high heat.

Grill for 15-20 minutes, or until done.

Baste with the honey and vinegar mixture while cooking.

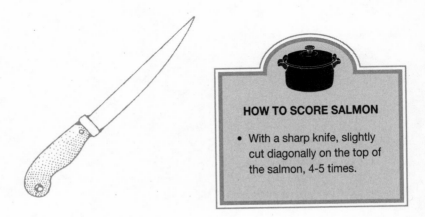

HOW TO SCORE SALMON

- With a sharp knife, slightly cut diagonally on the top of the salmon, 4-5 times.

Halibut with Fresh Herbs

—MAKES 2 SERVINGS—

The fresh herbs add a wonderful flavor to the halibut.

1 pound fresh halibut
1 tablespoon extra virgin olive oil
1 tablespoon fresh lemon juice
1 teaspoon lemon zest
1 teaspoon chopped fresh rosemary
1 teaspoon chopped fresh parsley
1 teaspoon chopped fresh basil
1/8 teaspoon red pepper flakes
1/2 teaspoon garlic, minced
1/4 teaspoon salt
Fresh ground pepper

In a small bowl, combine the olive oil, lemon juice, lemon zest, herbs, pepper flakes, garlic, salt and pepper.

Rub this mixture over the halibut and let it sit for 20 minutes.

Place the halibut on the barbeque grill and cook it over medium-high heat for 20 minutes or until done.

The halibut can also be baked in a 400°F oven for 15-20 minutes.

Halibut with Panko Breading

—MAKES 2 SERVINGS—

I received this recipe from my Jazzercise instructor, Phyllis.
It's a favorite of mine when halibut is in season.

1 pound halibut steaks
2 tablespoons stone-ground or Dijon mustard
2 tablespoons finely chopped fresh Italian parsley
¼ teaspoon salt
Fresh ground pepper
½ cup panko bread crumbs (Japanese-style bread crumbs)

Preheat oven to 450°F.

Prepare a casserole dish with nonstick cooking spray.

In a medium bowl, combine the mustard, parsley, salt and pepper.

Spread the mustard over both sides of the fish.

Place the panko on a plate and coat both sides of the halibut with the bread crumbs.

Bake for 10-15 minutes or until done.

Oven~Baked Fish

—MAKES 2 SERVINGS—

I like to serve this with Oven-Baked Potato Wedges (page 123)
and homemade tartar sauce.

1 pound white fish, such as tilapia, cod, halibut or sole
1 ½ cups crushed soda crackers (low-sodium, wheat)
½ teaspoon dried dill weed
2 tablespoons Italian salad dressing

Preheat oven to 450°F.

Spray a casserole dish with nonstick spray.

Rinse the fish and pat it dry.

Mix together the cracker crumbs and dill and place on a plate.

Pour the salad dressing onto another plate.

Roll each fillet first in the dressing and then into the cracker-crumb mixture.

Place the fish in the casserole dish and fold the thin ends under the fish.

Bake until fish begins to flake easily — 4-6 minutes per ½-inch of thickness.

Prawns with Cilantro and Lime

I serve this seafood dish with brown rice.

Sprinkle a little cilantro over the rice to tie in the flavors.

Try using different herbs, such as Italian parsley, rosemary or mint.

1 pound large prawns, peeled
2 tablespoons fresh lime juice
1 teaspoon lime zest
1 clove garlic, pressed
1 tablespoon finely chopped cilantro
2 tablespoons olive oil
¼ teaspoon salt
Fresh ground pepper

Squeeze the lime into a glass measuring cup. Add the lime zest, garlic, cilantro, olive oil, salt and pepper.

In a large ziploc bag, add the peeled prawns and the lime juice mixture.

Refrigerate for 1 hour.

Thread the marinated prawns onto shish kebab skewers and barbeque over medium-high heat, 2-3 minutes on each side.

These can also be cooked in a frying pan.

Rosemary Garlic Prawns

—MAKES 2 SERVINGS—

These prawns are great on shish kebab skewers. The marinade can also be used with chicken.

1 pound large prawns (13-15 count is best)
2 tablespoons olive oil
2 tablespoons lemon juice
½ teaspoon lemon zest
1 tablespoon fresh chopped rosemary, or ½ teaspoon dried
2 garlic cloves, minced
¼ teaspoon salt
Fresh ground black pepper

Peel the shrimp and place them in a ziploc bag.

In a small bowl, combine the oil, lemon juice, lemon zest, rosemary, minced garlic, salt and pepper. Pour over the prawns and marinate for 1 hour.

Thread the prawns onto 4 metal or wooden skewers. If you use wood, soak them in water for 15 minutes (before adding the prawns).

Grill the prawns, turning as each side browns. Total cooking time will be about 8 minutes.

Salmon in White Wine

The sweetness of the brown sugar makes this dish delicious. It's a great recipe for the barbeque, but this salmon can also be baked in the oven.

1 pound fresh wild salmon
2 tablespoons lowfat mayonnaise
2 tablespoons nonfat plain yogurt
4 tablespoons brown sugar
$2/3$ cup white wine (chardonnay or pinot grigio)
1 large piece of heavy-duty aluminum foil

In a small bowl, combine the mayonnaise and yogurt.

Place the salmon in the middle of the foil. Spread the mayonnaise mixture over the top of the fish. Sprinkle the brown sugar over the top. Double-fold the foil and seal one end. Pour the wine into the other end and seal.

Barbeque over medium-high heat, 15-20 minutes or until done.

If baking, preheat oven to 350°F and bake for 25-30 minutes.

Salmon with Garlic Paste

—MAKES 2 SERVINGS—

Garlic is good in everything, even salmon.

1 pound fresh wild salmon
2 cloves garlic, minced
½ teaspoon dried dill
½ teaspoon salt
1 teaspoon lemon juice
½ teaspoon lemon zest
Fresh ground pepper

Preheat oven to 400°F.

Place the garlic, dill, salt, lemon juice, lemon zest and pepper into a mortar or blender. Mix with the pestle or blend until you create a paste.

Place the salmon in an oven-proof dish that has been prepared with nonstick spray.

Rub the paste over the top of the salmon.

Bake for 20-25 minutes or until done.

Sea Scallops with Lime

—MAKES 2 SERVINGS—

I mixed large prawns in with the scallops;
it was a wonderful combination.

2 tablespoons olive oil
1 pound fresh large sea scallops
¼ cup white wine
2 tablespoons fresh lime juice
1 teaspoon lime zest
1 clove garlic, minced
1 tablespoon finely chopped cilantro
¼ teaspoon salt
Fresh ground pepper
2 tablespoons fresh flat-leaf parsley,
    chopped

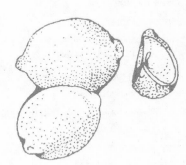

Rinse the scallops and pat dry.

**Heat a large nonstick frying pan over medium-high heat. Add the oil and sea
scallops. Cook on each side until a caramelized crust appears, about 3-5
minutes per side.**

Remove the scallops from the pan and set aside.

**Turn the heat down to medium. Add the white wine, lime juice, lime zest,
minced garlic, cilantro, salt and pepper.**

**Reduce by half and add the scallops. Continue to cook until the scallops are
done, about 2 minutes. Do not overcook.**

Top with the parsley.

Sole with Capers and Olives

—MAKES 4 SERVINGS—

I like to serve this dish with brown rice and a green vegetable.

1 1/4 pounds Dover sole, tilapia or cod
1/4 cup chopped kalamata olives
2 tablespoons capers, rinsed
1 14.5-ounce can diced tomatoes
1/4 cup chopped onion or shallot
1 teaspoon fresh rosemary, chopped
2 cloves garlic, minced
1/4 cup white wine (chardonnay or pinot grigio)
1/2 teaspoon salt
Fresh ground pepper
Double-folded aluminum foil

Preheat oven to 400°F.

In a medium bowl, combine the olives, capers, tomatoes, onion, rosemary, garlic, wine, salt and pepper.

Place fish in the middle of the foil. Spread the tomato mixture on top. Double-fold the foil and seal the ends.

Bake for 13 minutes or until done.

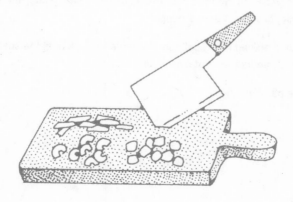

Soy~Ginger Salmon

—MAKES 2 SERVINGS—

This works well on the barbeque.

1 pound fresh, wild salmon
$^2/_3$ cup low-sodium soy sauce
1 tablespoon chopped fresh ginger
1 large piece of heavy-duty aluminum foil

Preheat oven to 400°F.

Place the salmon, soy sauce, and ginger in a ziploc bag and marinate for 1 hour.

Prepare a casserole dish with nonstick spray.

Place the salmon mixture in the dish.

Bake for 15-20 minutes or until done.

TO BARBEQUE

Place salmon mixture in the middle of the foil. Double-fold the foil and seal the ends.

Cook salmon for 10-15 minutes over medium-high heat or until done.

Tilapia with Rosemary-Ginger Rub

This fish dish goes well with Oven-Baked Potato Wedges.
I serve it with a green salad and tartar sauce, of course.

1 pound tilapia fillets
Rosemary-ginger spice rub (I use Stubb's brand)

Preheat oven to 400°F.

Prepare a casserole dish with nonstick spray.

Rub the spice mixture over both sides of the fish and place it in the prepared dish. Bake for 10-15 minutes or until done.

Vegetables

Cooking locally-grown vegetables keeps us in touch with the seasons. The food tastes better, we are eating food at its peak, and it's less expensive.

Acorn Squash

To serve, I cut each squash half lengthwise into four pieces,
keeping the stem intact.

1 acorn squash, washed and cut in half lengthwise
1 tablespoon olive oil
½ teaspoon salt
Fresh ground black pepper
¼ cup grated Parmesan cheese

Preheat oven to 400°F.

Scoop out the seeds and membranes of the squash.

Place the squash into a baking dish, cut side down.

Pour ½ cup water into the bottom of the dish.

Bake uncovered for 30-40 minutes or until tender.

Discard the water.

Turn the squash flesh side up.

Brush the top with the olive oil, salt, pepper and cheese.

Broil until golden brown.

Artichokes with Yogurt Dipping Sauce

—MAKES 2 SERVINGS—

These artichokes have a delicious flavor all on their own.
Try serving melted butter or yogurt dipping sauce (page 118) for variety.

2 medium artichokes
1 large clove garlic, pressed
½ teaspoon salt

Cut ½ inch off the top of each artichoke. Cut off the base and remove the small outer leaves near the bottom. Soak the artichokes in cold water until clean.

Place the artichokes in a large pan with the stem down. Pour an inch of water into the pan and salt to taste, about 1 teaspoon.

Add the garlic and place a lid on the pan. Bring to a boil.

Reduce heat to low and steam for 25-30 minutes. Artichokes are done when the leaves come off easily.

Drain artichokes and place them on individual plates.

When you get down to the small leaves and hair, gently remove these and discard. The heart at the base is the best part.

Caramelized Mushrooms in White Wine

—MAKES 4 SERVINGS—

Crimini mushrooms are related to white mushrooms, but they are more flavorful. The portobello mushroom is a mature crimini mushroom.

1 tablespoon butter
1 tablespoon olive oil
½ sweet onion, cut into 1-inch pieces
½ teaspoon salt
Fresh ground black pepper
1 pound crimini mushrooms, cleaned and cut in half
1 teaspoon lemon juice
¼ teaspoon lemon zest
¼-⅓ cup white wine

In a medium frying pan, melt the butter.

Add the oil, onion, salt and pepper. Cook over medium-high heat for 5 minutes or until onions start to turn brown.

Add the mushrooms, lemon juice and zest. Cook for 5-10 more minutes, or until the mushrooms turn light brown.

Add the wine and reduce to desired consistency.

Cauliflower Mash

—MAKES 4 SERVINGS—

This is a vegetable dish kids will love.
The Parmesan cheese and garlic add some good flavor.

1 tablespoon canola oil
2-3 garlic cloves, chopped
1 medium cauliflower, cleaned and broken into large pieces
1 cup chicken broth
1/4-1/2 cup grated Parmesan cheese
2 tablespoons fresh chopped Italian parsley
1/2 teaspoon salt
Fresh ground black pepper

Heat a medium saucepan over medium-high heat.

Add the oil and garlic. Cook for 1 minute.

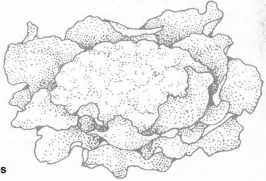

Add the cauliflower and chicken broth. Bring to a boil.

Cover the pan, reduce the heat to simmer, and cook for 15-20 minutes or until the cauliflower is soft.

Remove half the liquid in the pan and set it aside.

Mash the cauliflower to a desired consistency, adding the reserved liquid as needed.

Gently fold in the Parmesan cheese.

Season to taste.

Sprinkle with chopped parsley.

Fall Harvest Green Beans

—MAKES 2 SERVINGS—

This recipe is a great way to use the fall vegetables still in your garden.
For a tasty alternative, try using zucchini instead of the green beans.

2 teaspoons extra virgin olive oil
1/2 medium sweet onion, sliced thin
1/2 teaspoon salt
Fresh ground black pepper
1/2 pound cooked fresh green beans, cut into 1-inch pieces
1 cup chopped fresh tomatoes
1/2 teaspoon dried oregano
2 cloves garlic, minced
2 teaspoons balsamic vinegar
1/4 cup fresh basil, chopped

Heat a large frying pan over medium-high heat. Add the oil, onion, salt and pepper and cook for 3 minutes.

Add the green beans, tomatoes, oregano and garlic.
Cook for 1 minute.

Add the vinegar and basil, and cook for another minute.

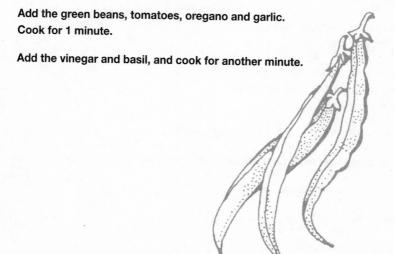

Italian Zucchini Bake

You can buy the roasted tomatoes or roast them yourself (page 105).

2 8-inch green or yellow zucchini, cut into ½-inch thick rounds
6 roasted tomato slices, chopped
½ onion, sliced
2 tablespoons olive oil
2 garlic cloves, minced
5 kalamata olives, chopped
½ teaspoon salt
Fresh ground black pepper
2 tablespoons grated Parmesan cheese

Preheat oven to 450°F.

In a large bowl, combine the zucchini, tomato, onion, oil, garlic, olives, salt and pepper.

Pour into an 8-inch square pan prepared with nonstick spray.

Sprinkle the cheese on top.

Bake for 15 minutes.

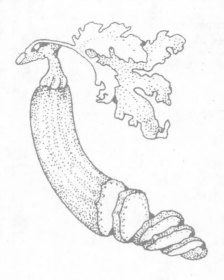

Lemon Asparagus

—MAKES 4 SERVINGS—

Pencil-thin asparagus works best in this recipe. You can either pan-fry these or grill them on the barbeque. Try using different varieties of citrus fruit, such as orange or grapefruit.

2 teaspoons extra virgin olive oil
1 small shallot, finely chopped
2 cloves garlic, minced
1 pound asparagus, cleaned and trimmed
½ teaspoon salt
Fresh ground black pepper
2 tablespoons fresh lemon juice
1 teaspoon lemon zest

Heat a sauté pan over medium-high heat.

Add the oil and shallot and sauté for 2 minutes.

Add the garlic and sauté for 1 minute.

Add the asparagus, salt and pepper and cook, stirring often, for an additional 3-4 minutes.

Add the lemon juice and zest, and cook for an additional minute.

Roasted Butternut Squash

The butternut squash is a winter squash and comes from the gourd family.

1 8-to-12-inch butternut squash
1/4 cup extra virgin olive oil
1 teaspoon salt
Fresh ground black pepper
1/2 teaspoon Hungarian paprika
1/2 teaspoon ground cloves
1/4 teaspoon freshly grated or dried nutmeg
1/4 cup freshly grated Parmesan cheese

Preheat oven to 375°F.

Grease a 9x11-inch casserole dish with nonstick spray.

Wash the squash and cut it into 1-inch rounds.

Scoop out the seeds and cut off the peel with a paring knife.

Rub both sides of the squash rings with oil and place in the prepared pan.

In a small bowl, combine the salt, pepper, paprika, cloves, nutmeg and cheese. Sprinkle over the top of the squash.

Drizzle the remaining oil over the top and bake for 1 hour.

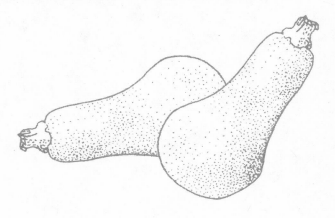

Roasted Cauliflower with Olives

—MAKES 4 SERVINGS—

Roasted vegetables make an ideal accompaniment to chicken or fish dishes. You can also toss them with pasta and Parmesan cheese.

1 medium cauliflower, cleaned and cut into 2-inch wide florets
4 tablespoons olive oil
4 cloves garlic, minced
½ teaspoon salt
Fresh ground pepper
10 kalamata olives, chopped

Preheat oven to 425°F.

Combine all the ingredients in a large bowl.

Arrange cauliflower mixture on a baking dish.

Bake on the top rack of the oven for 25 minutes or until the cauliflower is caramelized and soft when pierced with a knife.

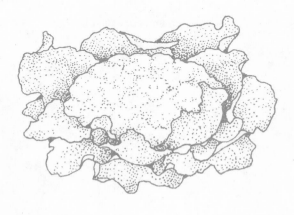

Roasted Tomatoes

6 Roma tomatoes, cut in half lengthwise
2 tablespoons olive oil
1 tablespoon fresh thyme
2 cloves garlic, minced
½ teaspoon salt
Fresh ground black pepper

Preheat oven to 450°F.

Prepare a cookie sheet with nonstick cooking spray or line it with parchment paper.

Remove seeds and stems from the tomatoes.

Place them cut-side up on a cookie sheet.

Drizzle olive oil over the top.

Place the thyme, garlic, salt and pepper on top of each tomato.

Roast for 30 minutes or until the tomatoes turn brown.

Sautéed Beet Greens

—MAKES 2 SERVINGS—

Beet greens have a lot of flavor and vitamins.
The best ones are young and tender.

Leaves from 4 medium beets, washed and stems removed
1 teaspoon olive oil
1 teaspoon butter
¼ teaspoon salt
Fresh ground black pepper
2-3 tablespoons balsamic vinegar

Heat a large frying pan over medium-high heat.

Add the oil, butter, beet leaves, salt and pepper.

Sauté for 4 minutes.

Drizzle the vinegar along the outside of the leaves and cook for an additional 4 minutes.

Sesame Spinach

Try adding caramelized onions to this dish — it's delicious.

1 pound fresh spinach, washed and dried
1 tablespoon sesame oil
2 cloves garlic, minced
½ teaspoon salt
Fresh ground black pepper
2 teaspoons lemon juice
½ teaspoon lemon zest
1 tablespoon sesame seeds

Heat a large frying pan over medium-high heat.

Add the oil, garlic, spinach, salt and pepper.

Cook for 3-4 minutes or until spinach is almost done.

Add the lemon juice and zest, and cook for an additional minute.

Serve with the sesame seeds sprinkled over the top.

Spinach with Balsamic Vinegar

—MAKES 2 SERVINGS—

Serve this on individual plates with thinly sliced roasted beets around the edges.

2 teaspoons canola oil
1 pound fresh spinach, washed and dried
2 tablespoons balsamic vinegar

Heat a large frying pan over medium-high heat.

Add the oil and spinach. Cook for 3-4 minutes or until almost done.

Stir in the balsamic vinegar and cook until the vinegar is reduced.

Swiss Chard

This is a good vegetable to serve with fish and rice.

2 teaspoons extra virgin olive oil
1 small shallot, finely chopped
2 cloves garlic, minced
¼ teaspoon salt
Fresh ground black pepper
1 bunch Swiss chard, washed
1 tablespoon raspberry vinegar
⅛ teaspoon fresh ground nutmeg

Remove the stems and veins from the Swiss chard and cut it into 1-inch pieces.

Heat a large frying pan over medium-high heat.

Add the oil, shallot, garlic, salt and pepper. Cook for 1 minute.

Add the Swiss chard and cook until wilted, 3 to 4 minutes.

Add the vinegar and nutmeg, and cook for an additional minute.

Vegetable Stir Fry

—MAKES 8 SERVINGS—

This recipe is versatile. Try using different mushrooms and vegetables.
Add leftover cooked chicken and serve over brown rice.

1 ½ teaspoons sesame oil

2 carrots, peeled and cut diagonally into ¼-inch-thick slices

2 cups button or crimini mushrooms, sliced

½ teaspoon salt

Fresh ground pepper

2 cups fresh asparagus, cut diagonally into 1-inch slices

2 cups pea pods

1 tablespoon fresh ginger, minced

2 teaspoons reduced-sodium soy sauce

1 tablespoon toasted sesame seeds

Heat a large frying pan over medium-high heat. Add the oil, carrots, mushrooms, salt and pepper. Stir-fry for 6 minutes.

Add the asparagus, pea pods and ginger, and stir-fry for another 3 minutes.

Add the soy sauce and cook for an additional minute.

Place in a serving bowl and top with sesame seeds.

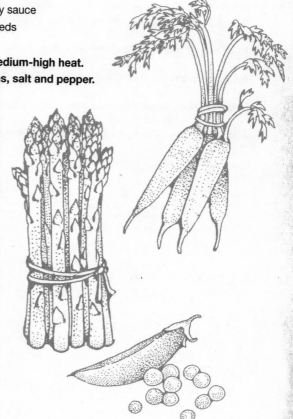

Zucchini and Green Chiles

—MAKES 8 SERVINGS—

The green chiles add a nice kick to this dish.

1-2 tablespoons canola oil
1 medium onion, chopped
2 medium green zucchini, cut into ½-inch slices
2 medium yellow zucchini, cut into ½-inch slices
½ teaspoon salt
Fresh ground black pepper
2 clove garlic, minced
1 cup corn (canned, frozen or fresh off the cob)
1 4-ounce can diced mild green chiles, undrained

Heat a large frying pan over medium-high heat.

Add the canola oil and onion, and cook for 10 minutes.

Add the sliced zucchini, salt and pepper, and cook for an additional minute.

Add the garlic and cook for an additional minute.

Add the corn and green chiles and bring to a boil.

Reduce heat and simmer for 5 minutes.

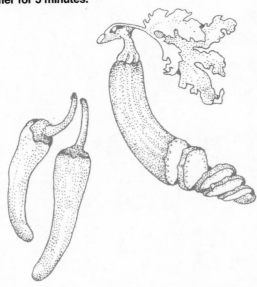

Zucchini Stir Fry

—MAKES 4 SERVINGS—

This dish is easy to prepare and is a good way to use zucchini.

2 teaspoons olive oil
1 teaspoon butter
1 medium-size sweet onion, chopped
½ teaspoon salt
Fresh ground black pepper
1 pound yellow or green zucchini, sliced in half
   lengthwise and then into ¼-inch slices
½ teaspoon fresh lemon juice
½ teaspoon lemon zest
2 cloves garlic, minced

Heat a large frying pan over medium-high heat.

Add the oil, butter, onion, salt and pepper. Cook for 10 minutes or until caramelized.

Add the zucchini, lemon juice and lemon zest. Cook for another 2-3 minutes.

Add the garlic and cook for 1 more minute.

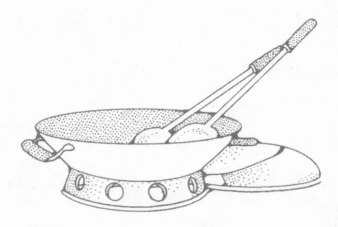

Sauces

I grew up in a family where everyone loved to dip their food. Whether it was fish into tartar sauce, fresh-cracked crab into secret sauce or pork chops into homemade applesauce, we sure enjoyed our sauces.

Applesauce

—MAKES 5-6 CUPS—

A food mill is a tool used to purée food. I use mine for applesauce and to make creamy mashed potatoes.

3 pounds washed apples (McIntosh, Golden Delicious, Galas, Jonagolds)
1 cup water
2 tablespoons fresh lemon juice
Sugar, honey or Splenda, to taste
½ teaspoon allspice
1 teaspoon ground cinnamon

Peel and core apples and cut into 1-inch pieces.

Place the apples, water and lemon juice in a large saucepan.

Bring the liquid to a boil over high heat and cover.

Reduce heat to medium and cook, stirring occasionally for 30-40 minutes or until apples are soft.

Remove from the heat and cool.

Purée the cooled apples in a blender or run them through a food mill.

Pour the puréed apples back into the saucepan.

Add the sugar, cinnamon and allspice.

Simmer for 5-10 minutes.

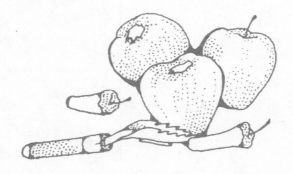

Pesto

*This is great to have already prepared in the freezer. I like to pull a
cube or two out and use them with grilled shrimp, pasta, clams or soups.
Try using edamame instead of herbs.*

1 bunch Italian parsley
1 bunch basil
1 bunch cilantro
½ cup canola oil
2 tablespoons lemon juice
1 teaspoon lemon zest
2 cloves garlic
½ cup lightly toasted nuts
   (pine nuts, pecans, walnuts, pistachios, almonds, or hazelnuts)
½ cup grated Parmesan cheese
½ teaspoon salt

Choose any combination of herbs; wash and coarsely chop them.

Purée all ingredients in a food processor or blender until blended.

Keep chilled or freeze in ice cube trays.
Pesto keeps well in the freezer for up to 6 months.

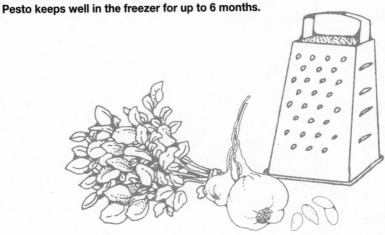

Secret Sauce

—MAKES 2 CUPS—

I serve this with crab or prawns as a dip.
My daughter Lisa always asks for it.

1 ¼ cups lowfat mayonnaise
    or ½ cup nonfat plain yogurt and ¾ cup lowfat mayonnaise
⅓ cup chili sauce
2 tablespoons Dijon mustard
2 tablespoons rinsed capers
⅛ teaspoon hot pepper sauce
3-4 tablespoons ketchup

Combine the above ingredients in a medium bowl and chill for 2-3 hours.

Add as much hot pepper sauce as you like.

Sour Cream Sauce with Capers

Serve this sauce over fish or chicken.

1 tablespoon olive oil
1 clove garlic, minced
¼ cup lemon juice
½ teaspoon lemon zest
2 tablespoons capers, rinsed
Salt and lemon pepper, to taste
½ cup fat-free or light sour cream

Heat a small frying pan over medium-high heat.

Add the olive oil and garlic.

Cook for 1 minute.

Add the lemon juice, lemon zest, capers, sour cream, salt and pepper.

Simmer for 5 minutes.

Tartar Sauce

—MAKES 1/2 CUP—

¼ cup reduced-fat mayonnaise
¼ cup plain lowfat yogurt
2 tablespoons finely chopped dill pickle
1 tablespoon finely chopped onion
1 teaspoon chopped fresh parsley

Mix all ingredients in a small bowl and chill.

Yogurt Dipping Sauce

MAKES 1/3 CUP

I use this as a dipping sauce for artichokes or any fresh vegetable.

2 tablespoons lowfat mayonnaise
2 tablespoons fat-free plain yogurt
½ teaspoon fresh lemon juice
1 small garlic clove, pressed
1-2 teaspoons Worcestershire sauce

In a small bowl, combine all the ingredients and refrigerate.

Sides

Most people think of an entrée first when they are planning a meal. Side dishes can be a great way to add fiber, variety and color, and often become the favorite part of a meal.

Bhutanese Red Rice Pilaf

—MAKES 4 SERVINGS—

Bhutanese red rice is ancient short-grain rice grown at 8,000 feet in the Himalayan Kingdom of Bhutan.

1 cup red rice (Bhutanese), sorted and rinsed
1 tablespoon butter
1 tablespoon canola oil
2 tablespoons finely chopped shallot
1/8 teaspoon salt
Fresh ground pepper
1/2 cup finely chopped carrot
1/2 cup chopped shiitake mushrooms
1 1/2 cups chicken stock
1 bay leaf
Sprig of fresh thyme

Preheat oven to 450°F.

Heat a large ovenproof saucepan over medium-high heat.

Add the butter, oil, shallot, salt and pepper. Cook for 2 minutes, or until shallot is soft.

Add the carrots, mushrooms and rice. Sauté for one minute.

Add the chicken stock, bay leaf and thyme. Bring to a boil and cover.

Place the saucepan in the oven and bake for 15 minutes or until the rice is done.

Remove from the oven, uncover and fluff the rice with a fork.

Remove the bay leaf and thyme stem.

Transfer to a warmed serving bowl. Salt and pepper to taste.

Black-Eyed Peas

—MAKES 6 SERVINGS—

Black-eyed peas are supposed to bring good luck if eaten on New Year's Day.

½ cup dried (or 1 15-ounce can)
   black-eyed peas, rinsed and sorted
4 slices bacon, ham or Canadian
   bacon, cut into ½-inch pieces
2 tablespoons olive oil
4 cups chopped fresh or frozen spinach
½ cup chopped onion
1 clove garlic, minced
½ cup chicken stock
Grated fresh nutmeg, or ⅛ teaspoon
   dried
⅛ teaspoon sage
1 tablespoon fresh chopped parsley
2 tablespoons olive oil
½ teaspoon salt
Fresh ground pepper

Cook the dried peas as directed on the package.

Cook the bacon until almost done.

Remove from the pan and drain the bacon on a paper towel.

Heat a 3-quart saucepan over medium-high heat. Add 1 tablespoon olive oil and sauté the spinach until wilted. (If using frozen spinach, defrost and squeeze out the liquid.)

Remove spinach from the pan and set aside.

Add the remaining olive oil and heat over medium-high heat.

Add the onion and cook until tender, about 5 minutes.

Add the garlic and cook for 1 minute.

Add the bacon, spinach, black-eyed peas, chicken stock and spices to the pan and stir. Season with salt and pepper and bring to a boil.

Reduce the heat and cook until the chicken stock is reduced by half. Season to taste.

HOW TO PREPARE BEANS

- Soak beans in water for 8-10 hours. Drain.

  Place beans and 1 tsp. salt in a large pot. Cover with water about 1 inch above the beans.

- Bring to a boil and partially cover. Boil gently until tender, about 1 ½ to 2 hours. Add hot water as needed to keep beans just covered with liquid.

- Test frequently during cooking, and come to your own decision about when beans are tender.

Mashed Yams with Rosemary and Toasted Hazelnuts

—MAKES 4 SERVINGS—

Who can resist a great potato dish?
This one is not only healthy, but colorful too.

2 pounds peeled yams or sweet potatoes, cubed
¼ cup chicken broth
1 teaspoon chopped fresh rosemary
½ teaspoon salt
Fresh ground pepper
¼ cup toasted hazelnuts, chopped

Place yams in a medium saucepan and cover with water. Add ½ teaspoon salt and bring to a boil.

Reduce heat to medium and cook for 10 minutes or until soft when pierced with a knife. Remove from heat and drain.

Return the yams to the saucepan and add the broth and rosemary.

Mash yams. Salt and pepper to taste.

Serve with the chopped hazelnuts sprinkled on top.

HOW TO TOAST HAZELNUTS

- Preheat oven to 200°F.

- Spread the hazelnuts onto a baking sheet and toast in the preheated oven for 6-10 minutes, or until the skins have loosened.

- Remove from the oven and allow to cool slightly.

- Remove the skins by rubbing the nuts in the corner of a tea towel.

- If they are not sufficiently toasted, return them to the oven until they become golden brown.

- Chop the hazelnuts and set aside for garnish.

Oven~Baked Potato Wedges*

—MAKES 6 SERVINGS—

Any type of potato works for this recipe. Try using different spices.

6 Yukon Gold potatoes
2 tablespoons canola oil
1/3 cup grated Parmesan cheese
2 teaspoons Hungarian paprika
Pinch red pepper flakes
Salt and pepper

Preheat oven to 375°F.

Cut each potato into wedges.

In a large bowl, combine the potatoes, canola oil, cheese, paprika, salt and pepper. Place the potatoes in a casserole dish that has been prepared with nonstick spray.

Bake for 1 hour.

* *Recipe adapted from* "Simply Classic" *by The Junior League of Seattle.*

Roasted Potatoes

—MAKES 4 SERVINGS—

You can use a combination of any potatoes. I like to mix up the colors.

4 Yukon Gold, red or sweet potatoes, cleaned and cut into ½-inch cubes
1 sweet onion, cut into ½-inch pieces
1-2 tablespoons olive oil
2 tablespoons chopped Italian parsley
½ teaspoon salt
Fresh ground pepper
½ cup sour cream
2 tablespoons chopped chives

Preheat oven to 450°F.

Prepare a casserole dish with nonstick spray.

In a large bowl, mix together the potatoes, onion, oil, parsley, salt and pepper.

Place this into the casserole dish and bake for 35-40 minutes or until brown.

Serve with sour cream and chives.

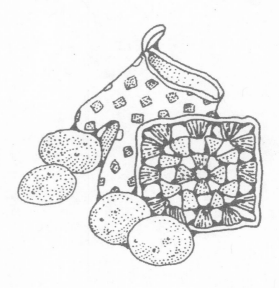

Scalloped Potatoes

This beautiful dish combines creamy potatoes with a bubbly, creamy sauce. It's delicious and simple to make.

6 large potatoes (Yukon Gold, red or purple), peeled and sliced into $1/4$-inch rounds
1 medium onion, sliced thin
1 teaspoon salt
Fresh ground black pepper
3 cups grated, medium cheddar cheese
1 10 $3/4$-ounce can Healthy Request® Cream of Mushroom soup
1 cup fat-free milk
$1/8$ teaspoon freshly grated nutmeg
2 tablespoons fresh chopped parsley

Preheat oven to 350°F.

Prepare a 9x11-inch baking dish with nonstick spray.

In a medium bowl, combine the soup and milk.

Layer half of the potatoes in the bottom of the baking dish.

Place half of the onions on top. Add $1/2$ teaspoon salt and pepper to taste.

Sprinkle on half of the cheese and half of the nutmeg.

Pour half of the soup mixture over the top.

Repeat the process and top with the chopped parsley.

Cover the dish with aluminum foil.

Bake for 90 minutes or until potatoes are soft.

Sweet Potato Casserole

I like to serve this dish when I'm looking for ways to add fiber.
There are four grams of fiber in a small sweet potato.

4 sweet potatoes, skinned and cut into 1-inch cubes
1 sweet onion, chopped
⅛ teaspoon ground cloves
⅛ teaspoon ground cinnamon
Cayenne pepper, to taste
½ teaspoon fresh thyme, or ⅛ teaspoon dried
½ teaspoon salt
Fresh ground pepper
½ cup chicken stock
1 tablespoon fresh chopped parsley

Preheat oven to 375°F.

Prepare a casserole dish with nonstick spray.

Place the cubed sweet potatoes and onion in the dish.

Mix in the cloves, cinnamon, cayenne pepper, thyme, salt and pepper.

Pour the chicken stock on top and bake with the lid on for 20 minutes.

Remove the lid and bake for another 20-25 minutes or until potatoes are soft.

Top with the parsley.

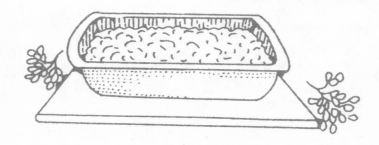

Twice-Baked Potatoes

—MAKES 2 SERVINGS—

My daughter Lisa, who is a terrific cook, created this recipe.
Everyone in the family loves these potatoes.

2 large russet potatoes, scrubbed
2 garlic cloves, minced
½ teaspoon salt
Fresh ground pepper, to taste
½ to 1 cup warm milk, (skim, 1% or fat-free half and half)
½ cup grated, low-fat cheddar cheese
¼ cup grated Romano cheese
½ cup light sour cream
3 tablespoons chopped chives
¼ cup grated Parmesan cheese

Preheat oven to 400°F.

Poke the potatoes with a knife and bake for 1 hour or until soft.

Remove the potatoes from the oven. Cool and cut ³/₄ inch off the top of each potato.

With a spoon, remove the soft potatoes from their skins. Be careful not to tear the skin.

Place the softened cooked potatoes into a large bowl. Add the garlic, salt, pepper and the milk. Mash until desired consistency is reached.

Stir in the cheddar cheese, Romano and sour cream. Fold in the chopped chives and season to taste.

Place the potato skins on a greased cookie sheet and spoon the mixture into their skins.

Sprinkle Parmesan cheese on top and bake for 30 minutes.

Place under the broiler for a few minutes to brown the tops.

White Beans with Rosemary

—MAKES 8 SERVINGS—

This can also be a great main dish. Serve with a green salad to complete the meal.

4 ½ cups cooked white beans
1 ⅔ cups diced fresh tomatoes
1 small onion, finely chopped
¼ cup finely chopped fresh flat-leaf parsley
1 teaspoon chopped fresh rosemary, or ½ teaspoon dried
3 cloves garlic, minced
½ teaspoon salt
Fresh ground pepper
4 small rosemary sprigs

Preheat oven to 425°F.

Prepare a 2-quart casserole dish with nonstick cooking spray.

In a large bowl, combine the beans, tomatoes, onion, parsley, rosemary, garlic, salt and pepper.

Pour the ingredients into the prepared pan and top with the rosemary sprigs.

Cover and bake for 15 minutes or until heated through.

Brown Rice with Dressing

—MAKES 4 SERVINGS—

This healthy side is wonderful served with any entrée. Have fun and add any of the combinations listed below or add your own creative touches.

1 cup brown rice
1 teaspoon canola oil
2 cups low-sodium chicken broth

DRESSING

3 tablespoons red wine vinegar
1 ½ tablespoons olive oil
⅛ teaspoon salt
Fresh ground pepper

HOW TO TENDERIZE BROWN RICE

- Soak rice in water for an hour or two before cooking.

Heat a heavy saucepan over medium-high heat. Add the oil and rice; cook for 2 minutes.

Add the chicken broth and bring to a boil.

Reduce the heat to medium-low, cover and cook until the liquid is evaporated, about 40-45 minutes.

Remove from heat and place the rice in a large serving bowl. Toss with the dressing.

Serve alone or add any ingredient combination listed below:

- Toasted slivered almonds, frozen thawed peas, sliced green onions, chopped yellow peppers, chopped parsley and red pepper flakes.

- Chopped toasted pistachios, a sectioned orange, fresh basil leaves, red onion, and grated orange zest.

- Chopped tomatoes and fresh basil.

- Golden raisins, toasted slivered almonds, fresh parsley.

Desserts

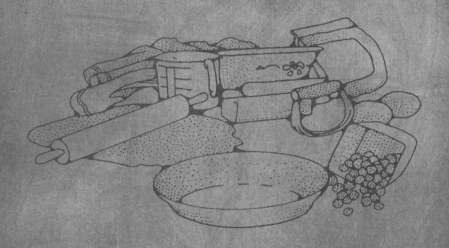

I always plan my parties thinking of the dessert first.
I then think of what would complement this course.
The smell of baked cookies or a peek at the coconut
angel cake will get your guests anticipating the meal.
Some of these recipes are low in fat and sugar, and
can be used to create a healthier finish to your meal.

Apple Walnut Cobbler

—MAKES 4 SERVINGS—

Try different types of apples in this recipe.

TOPPING

1 egg

¼ cup sugar

1 tablespoon melted butter

¼ cup fresh-squeezed orange juice

½ teaspoon orange zest

1 ⅓ cups oat flour

⅛ teaspoon salt

1 ½ teaspoons baking powder

½ teaspoon baking soda

In a medium bowl, lightly mix the egg and sugar.

Stir in the butter, orange juice and orange zest.

In another bowl, combine the flour, salt, baking powder, and baking soda.

Add it to the egg mixture and beat until smooth.

FILLING

2 large Gala apples, peeled, cored and thinly sliced

1 tablespoon fresh lemon juice

½ teaspoon lemon zest

2 tablespoons sugar

¼ teaspoon ground cinnamon

½ cup chopped walnuts

Preheat oven to 350°F.

Spray a pie pan with nonstick baking spray.

In a bowl, combine the sliced apples with the lemon juice, lemon zest, sugar and cinnamon.

Pour into the prepared pie pan.

Sprinkle the chopped walnuts over the top.

Bake for 20 minutes.

Remove from the oven and spoon the topping evenly over the cooked apples.

Bake for 25 minutes more or until done.

Brownies

The brownies taste best when served with a bowl of vanilla bean ice cream.

2/3 cup fat-free plain yogurt
1/2 cup cocoa powder
1 egg plus 1 egg white, slightly beaten
1 teaspoon vanilla
1 1/4 cups sugar
3/4 cup plus 2 tablespoons oat flour
1/4 teaspoon salt
1/2 cup chopped walnuts
1/2 cup chocolate chips

Preheat oven to 350°F.

Spray a 9x9-inch baking dish with nonstick cooking spray.

In a large bowl, combine the yogurt and cocoa. Mix well.

Add the eggs and mix until blended.

Stir in the vanilla.

Add the sugar and stir for 2 minutes with a whisk.

Gradually add the flour and salt, but do not overmix.

Fold in the walnuts.

Spread this batter onto the prepared pan and top with the chocolate chips.

Bake for 20-25 minutes or until a toothpick placed in the center comes out clean.

Place the baking pan on a cooling rack.

Cool completely and cut into squares.

Carrot Cake with Cream Cheese Frosting

—MAKES 24 SERVINGS—

This moist cake is a family favorite.

1 cup canola oil

2 cups sugar

4 eggs

2 cups all-purpose white flour

2 teaspoons baking powder

1 teaspoon baking soda

1 teaspoon ground cinnamon

1/2 teaspon salt

3 cups shredded carrots

1 cup chopped walnuts or pistachios

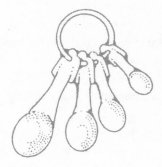

Preheat the oven to 300°F.

Grease and flour a 9x11-inch baking pan.

In a medium bowl, mix together the oil, sugar and eggs.

In a large bowl, stir together the flour, baking powder, baking soda, cinnamon and salt.

Pour the liquid ingredients into the flour mixture and mix well. Fold in the carrots and walnuts.

Place in the prepared pan and bake for 1 hour or until done.

Cool before frosting.

CREAM CHEESE FROSTING

1 8-ounce package cream cheese, room temperature

1/2 cup butter, room temperature

1 pound powdered sugar

1 teaspoon vanilla

1/2 cup chopped walnuts

In a large bowl, cream together the cream cheese, butter, sugar and vanilla.

Frost the cooled carrot cake and top with the walnuts.

Cheese and Fruit Platter

—MAKES 6-8 SERVINGS—

This dessert is a great way to end a dinner. It's fun to try different cheeses and use fruit that is in season. Have fun creating a piece of art with your platter.

3 different cheeses
a hard cheese, a soft creamy cheese, and a sharp-tasting cheese
Try varieties of cheddar, Swiss, Gouda, brie, goat, blue cheese.

Breads and crackers
Whole baguette, sliced rye, water wafers

Fruit
Grapes, fresh strawberries, kiwi

Nuts
Toasted almonds, macadamia nuts, pistachios

Garnishes
Any flat-leafed greens, parsley, hydrangeas

Chocolate
I like to chunk whole chocolate and serve it in a separate dish.

Equipment
A platter big enough to hold the cheese, bread, crackers, fruit and garnish.
Cheese knives.

Place the fruit in the middle of the platter. Group your cheese around this.

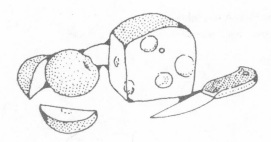

Coconut Angel Cake

My mother used to make this for birthdays when I was a child.
I make it now for my family and friends.

1 angel food cake mix
1 3.4-ounce coconut cream instant pudding mix
1 packet Dream Whip®
1 ½ cups milk
1 teaspoon vanilla
¼ cup coconut flakes
Fresh or frozen fruit (raspberries, blueberries, fresh peaches, blackberries)

Bake the angel food cake as directed.

Cool the cake and place it on a cake plate.

In a bowl, combine the coconut cream pudding, Dream Whip®, milk and the vanilla.

With a blender, mix for 2-3 minutes.

Place this in the refrigerator and chill.

Cut the cake in half, creating two layers.

Frost the first layer and place the second layer on top. Continue to frost the sides and the top.

Sprinkle the coconut on the top and sides.

Serve slices on individual plates with fruit spooned over each piece.

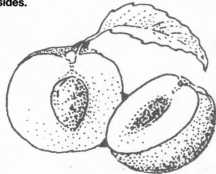

Fresh Berry Coffee Cake

—MAKE 12 SERVINGS—

I used to make this cake for camping trips as a special breakfast treat.
I served it with hard-boiled eggs and fruit.

$2/3$ cup butter, room temperature
1 $1/2$ cups sugar (1 $1/4$ cups for blueberries)
2 eggs
2 cups all-purpose flour
2 teaspoons baking powder
1 teaspoon salt
1 $1/2$ teaspoons ground cinnamon
$3/4$ cup milk
1 teaspoon vanilla
2 cups fresh blueberries, huckleberries or raspberries*
Whipping cream or Cool Whip®

Preheat the oven to 350°F.

In a large bowl, beat together the butter and 1 $1/4$ cups of the sugar (1 cup for the blueberries) until creamy.

Beat in the eggs, one at a time.

In another bowl, stir together the flour, baking powder, salt, and 1 teaspoon of the cinnamon.

Mix alternately with the milk into the butter mixture until batter is smooth.

Stir in the vanilla and the berries.

Spray a 9x13-inch baking dish with nonstick baking spray.

Pour the batter into the pan.

Mix the remaining $1/4$ cup sugar with $1/2$ teaspoon cinnamon and sprinkle over the batter. Bake for 40 minutes or until a toothpick inserted in the center comes out clean.

Top individual cake servings with the whipped cream or Cool Whip®.

* You can also use frozen, unsweetened berries, partially defrosted.

Iced Pumpkin Cookies

—MAKES 4 DOZEN—

These cookies are fun to decorate at Halloween.
I like to use orange sugar or sprinkles on top.

½ cup butter, room temperature
1 ½ cups sugar
1 cup pumpkin purée
1 egg
1 teaspoon vanilla
2 ½ cups oat flour
1 teaspoon baking powder
1 teaspoon baking soda
2 teaspoons ground cinnamon
½ teaspoon ground nutmeg
½ teaspoon ground cloves
½ teaspoon salt

FROSTING

1 8-ounce package cream cheese,
   room temperature
½ cup butter, room temperature
1 teaspoon vanilla

Beat together the cream cheese,
butter and vanilla in a medium bowl.

Ice the cookies with cream cheese
frosting.

Preheat oven to 350°F.

In a large bowl, cream the butter and
sugar.

Add the pumpkin purée, egg and
vanilla.

Gradually stir in the flour, baking
powder, baking soda, cinnamon,
nutmeg, cloves and salt.

Mix until blended.

Drop from a teaspoon onto a
greased cookie sheet, 2 inches apart.

Flatten slightly by using the back of a
fork dipped in cold water.

Bake for 12 minutes. Cool.

Pumpkin Pudding

This light dessert is beautiful served in chilled martini glasses.
I served it at Thanksgiving and it was a huge hit.

2 cups canned pumpkin purée
2 3.4-ounce boxes instant vanilla pudding (sugar-free pudding is okay, too)
3 cups skim milk
Chopped crystallized ginger
Whipped cream or French Vanilla Cool Whip®

Beat pudding mix into milk with wire whisk for 2 minutes.

Stir in the pumpkin purée.

Pour the pudding into separate serving bowls and top with the chopped ginger.

Cool in the refrigerator for a couple of hours.

Just before serving, top with whipped cream or Cool Whip®.

Ranger Cookies

—MAKES 3 DOZEN COOKIES—

I grew up with my Grandmother Biddy making these for her husband and grandchildren. She would double the recipe, refrigerate the dough and cook a dozen every day. Her house always smelled like cookies. Try adding 1/2 cup chocolate chips and 1/4 cup chopped walnuts. Yum.

1/2 cup butter, room temperature (1 cube)
3/4 cups sugar
1 egg
1/2 teaspoon vanilla
1 cup oat flour
1/2 teaspoon baking soda
1/4 teaspoon baking powder
1/4 teaspoon salt
1/2 teaspoon cinnamon
1/4 teaspoon nutmeg
1/2 cup coconut
1 cup old-fashioned oats
1 cup Rice Krispies®

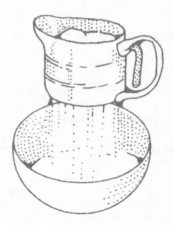

Preheat oven to 350°F.

In a large bowl, cream the butter and sugar.

Add the egg and vanilla. Mix until blended.

Gradually stir in the flour, baking soda, baking powder, salt, cinnamon and nutmeg.

Fold in the coconut, rolled oats and Rice Krispies®.

Chill dough for 30 minutes.

Using a tablespoon, drop dough two inches apart onto a greased cookie sheet.

Bake for 13 minutes. Cool on racks.

Wild Blackberry Cobbler

—MAKES 8 SERVINGS—

This recipe comes from Mrs. Pearl Thompson, my childhood Sunday
school teacher. I always serve this with vanilla ice cream.

3 cups wild blackberries
1 ¼ cups sugar
½ teaspoon ground cinnamon
1 tablespoon lemon juice
1 egg
¼ cup melted butter
1 teaspoon orange zest
½ cup fresh orange juice
1 ⅓ cups flour
1 ½ teaspoons baking powder
½ teaspoon soda
½ teaspoon salt

Preheat oven 350°F.

Combine berries and ½ cup sugar, cinnamon and lemon juice.

Turn this into a greased 9-inch-square baking dish.

Bake uncovered for 15 minutes.

In a large mixing bowl, beat the egg slightly.

Blend in the remaining ¾ cup sugar, butter, orange zest and juice.

In a medium bowl, stir together the flour, baking powder, soda and salt.

Add this to the egg mixture. Beat until smooth.

Remove the berries from the oven.

Spoon the batter evenly over the top.

Continue baking for another 30 minutes or until the cake springs back when lightly touched in the center.

INDEX

Acorn Squash, 96

Almonds, how to toast, 39

Appetizers, 13

Apple Walnut Cobbler, 132

Applesauce, 114
    as a fat substitute, 27

Artichokes with Yogurt Dipping Sauce, 97

Asparagus,
    Lemon Asparagus, 102
    Vegetable Stir Fry, 110

Avocado,
    Seafood Cobb Salad, 37
    Taco Salad, 41

Baked Lemon Salmon, 82

Balsamic Vinaigrette, 42

Banana Nut Bread, 22

Barbecued Pork, 14

Basic Vinaigrette, 42

Basil,
    Tomato Basil Soup, 50

Beans,
    Black-Eyed Peas, 121
    Chili, 59
    Fall Harvest Green Beans, 100
    How to prepare, 121
    Minestrone Soup, 46
    Southwest Chicken Chili, 53
    Tomato Basil Soup, 50
    White Beans with Rosemary, 128

Beef,
    Italian Meatballs, 66
    Marinated Flank Steak, 70
    Pot Roast and Gravy, 56

Beets,
    Roasted Beet Salad, 36
    Sautéed Beet Greens, 106

Berries,
    Blueberry Oat Bran Muffins, 23
    Fresh Berry Coffee Cake, 137
    Strawberry Spinach Salad, 40
    Wild Blackberry Cobbler, 141

Bhutanese Red Rice Pilaf, 120

Black-Eyed Peas, 121

Blanching, how to, 76

Blueberry Oat Bran Muffins, 23

Blue Cheese,
    Blue Cheese Dressing, 30
    Roasted Beet Salad, 36
    Seafood Cobb Salad, 37
    Spinach Salad with Chicken, 39
    Sweet Potato Salad, 35

Bran, 23

Breads, 21

Broth, how to strain, 44

Brown Rice with Dressing, 129

Brownies, 133

Bruschetta, 15

Buttermilk,
    Substitutions for, 25

INDEX

Cake,
    Carrot Cake with Cream Cheese
        Frosting, 134
    Coconut Angel Cake, 136
    Fresh Berry Coffee Cake, 137

Capers,
    Sour Cream Sauce with Capers, 117

Caprese Chop Salad, 31

Caramelized Mushrooms in White Wine, 98

Carrot,
    Carrot Cake with Cream Cheese
        Frosting, 134
    Pot Roast and Gravy, 56
    Zucchini Carrot Bread, 27

Carrot Cake with Cream Cheese Frosting, 134

Cauliflower,
    Cauliflower Mash, 99
    Roasted Cauliflower with Olives, 104

Celery Root,
    Chicken with Celery Root and Garlic, 52

Cheese,
    Bruschetta, 15
    Caprese Chop Salad, 31
    Chicken with Fresh Mozzarella
        and Noodles, 58
    Enchiladas, 61
    Fresh Pear and Gorgonzola Salad, 34
    Shrimp Corkscrew Salad, 38
    Taco Salad, 41
    Quiche, 73

Cheese and Fruit Platter, 135

Chicken,
    Chicken Curry Salad, 32
    Chicken Noodle Soup, 44
    Chicken Stir Fry with Peanut Sauce, 78
    Chicken Stock, 45
    Chicken with Celery Root and Garlic, 52
    Chicken with Fresh Mozzarella
        and Noodles, 58
    Enchiladas, 61
    One-Pot Italian Sausage and Potatoes, 71
    Paprika Chicken and Gravy, 65
    Roast Chicken with Citrus, 63
    Roast Chicken with Garlic, 62
    Stuffed Red Peppers, 76
    Southwest Chicken Chili, 53
    Spinach Salad with Chicken, 39

Chicken Curry Salad, 32

Chicken Noodle Soup, 44

Chicken Stir Fry with Peanut Sauce, 78

Chicken Stock, 45

Chicken with Celery Root and Garlic, 52

Chicken with Fresh Mozzarella
    and Noodles, 58

Chiles,
    Zucchini and Green Chiles, 111

Chili, 59
    Southwest Chicken Chili, 53

Chinese Egg Noodles with Shrimp, 33

Chocolate,
    Brownies, 133
    Cheese and Fruit Platter, 135

INDEX

Citrus,
Roast Chicken with Citrus, 63

Clams,
Seafood Stew, 48
Steamed Clams with Pesto Sauce, 19

Cobbler,
Wild Blackberry Cobbler, 141

Coconut Angel Cake, 136

Cookies,
Iced Pumpkin Cookies, 138
Ranger Cookies, 140

Corn,
Southwest Chicken Chili, 53
Sweet Corn Bread, 26

Crab,
Seafood Cobb Salad, 37

Cracker-Crumb Pork Chops, 60

Cranberries,
Fruit and Pumpkin Seed Bars, 24

Cream Cheese Frosting, 134

Deglaze, how to, 47

Desserts, 131

Deviled Eggs, 16

Dressing for Roast Turkey, 75

Eggs,
Deviled, 16
Quiche, 73
Sweet Potato Salad, 35

Enchiladas, 61

Entrées, 57

Fall Harvest Green Beans, 100

Fennel,
How to prepare, 48

Seafood Stew, 48

Fiber, 21, 50, 126

Fish, (see also Salmon)
Seafood Cobb Salad, 37
Seafood Stew, 48
Sole with Capers and Olives, 92
Halibut with Fresh Herbs, 84
Halibut with Panko Breading, 85
Oven-Baked Fish, 86
Tilapia with Rosemary-Ginger Rub, 94

Fresh Berry Coffee Cake, 137

Fresh Pear and Gorgonzola Salad, 34

Fruit and Pumpkin Seed Bars, 24

Gorgonzola,
Fresh Pear and Gorgonzola Salad, 34

Garlic,
Roast Chicken with Garlic, 62
Salmon with Garlic Paste, 90

Ginger,
Pumpkin Soup, 47
Soy-Ginger Salmon, 93
Tilapia with Rosemary-Ginger Rub, 94
Vegetable Stir Fry, 110

INDEX

Graham Bread, 25

Gravy, 56, 65

Greens,
    Black-Eyed Peas, 121
    Sautéed Beet Greens, 106
    Sesame Spinach, 107
    Spinach with Balsamic Vinegar, 108
    Swiss Chard, 109

Grilled Salmon, 83

Halibut,
    Seafood Stew, 48

Halibut with Fresh Herbs, 84

Halibut with Panko Breading, 85

Hamburgers — Mary's Style, 64

Hazelnuts,
    How to toast, 122
    Mashed Yams with Rosemary and
        Toasted Hazelnuts, 122

Herb Garden, 11

Hoisin Sauce, 70

Iced Pumpkin Cookies, 138

Irish Lamb Stew, 54

Italian Meatballs, 66

Italian Zucchini Bake, 101

Joe's Special, 67

Lamb,
    Irish Lamb Stew, 54
    Lamb Shish Kebab, 68

Lamb Shish Kebab, 68

Lemon Asparagus, 102

Lemon Vinaigrette, 42

Marinara Sauce, 69
    Chicken with Fresh Mozzarella
        and Noodles, 58

Marinated Flank Steak, 70

Mashed Yams with Rosemary and
    Toasted Hazelnuts, 122

Meat thermometer, how to use, 63

Meatloaf, Turkey, 79

Minestrone Soup, 46

Mushrooms,
    Bhutanese Red Rice Pilaf, 120
    Caramelized Mushrooms in White Wine, 98
    Chicken Stir Fry with Peanut Sauce, 78
    Joe's Special, 67
    Stuffed Mushrooms, 20
    Vegetable Stir Fry, 110

Mussels,
    Seafood Stew, 48

Mustard Sauce, hot, 14

Nuts,
    Apple Walnut Cobbler, 132
    Banana Nut Bread, 22

I N D E X

Nuts (continued),
 Brownies, 133
 Carrot Cake with Cream Cheese
  Frosting, 134
 Cheese and Fruit Platter, 135
 Chicken Curry Salad, 32
 Chicken Stir Fry with Peanut Sauce, 78
 Fresh Pear and Gorgonzola Salad, 34
 Pesto, 115
 Roasted Beet Salad, 36
 Toasted Walnuts, 36
 Zucchini Carrot Bread, 27

Olives,
 Roasted Cauliflower with Olives, 104
One-Pot Italian Sausage and Potatoes, 71
Onions, how to grate, 17
Oven-Baked Fish, 86
Oven-Baked Potato Wedges, 123

Paprika Chicken and Gravy, 65
Pasta,
 Chicken Noodle Soup, 44
 Chicken with Fresh Mozzarella
  and Noodles, 58
 Chinese Egg Noodles with Shrimp, 33
 Shrimp Corkscrew Salad, 38
Peanut Sauce, 78
Pears,
 Fresh Pear and Gorgonzola Salad, 34

Peas,
 Chicken Stir Fry with Peanut Sauce, 78
 Irish Lamb Stew, 54
 Shrimp Corkscrew Salad, 38
 Vegetable Stir Fry, 110
Peppers,
 How to blanch, 76
 Stuffed Red Peppers, 76
Pesto, 115
 Steamed Clams with Pesto Sauce, 19
Pork,
 Barbecued Pork, 14
 Black-Eyed Peas, 121
 Cracker-Crumb Pork Chops, 60
 Enchiladas, 61
 Italian Meatballs, 66
 Pork Roast with Sauerkraut, 55
 Pork Tenderloin, 72
Pork Roast with Sauerkraut, 55
Pork Tenderloin, 72
Pot Roast and Gravy, 56
Potatoes,
 Chicken with Celery Root and Garlic, 52
 Irish Lamb Stew, 54
 One-Pot Italian Sausage and Potatoes, 71
 Oven-Baked Potato Wedges, 123
 Pot Roast and Gravy, 56
 Roasted Potatoes, 124
 Scalloped Potatoes, 125
 Sweet Potato Salad, 35
 Twice-Baked Potatoes, 127

INDEX

Potatoes, Sweet
    Irish Lamb Stew, 54
    Mashed Yams with Rosemary and
        Toasted Hazelnuts, 122
    One-Pot Italian Sausage and Potatoes, 71
    Sweet Potato Casserole, 126
    Sweet Potato Salad, 35

Prawns,
    Marinara Sauce, 69
    Prawns with Cilantro and Lime, 87
    Rosemary Garlic Prawns, 88

Prawns with Cilantro and Lime, 87

Pumpkin,
    Iced Pumpkin Cookies, 138
    Pumpkin Pudding, 139
    Pumpkin Soup, 47

Pumpkin Pudding, 139

Pumpkin Soup, 47

Quiche, 73

Ranger Cookies, 140

Raspberry Vinaigrette, 42

Reducing liquid, how to, 52

Rice,
    Bhutanese Red Rice Pilaf, 120
    Brown Rice with Dressing, 129
    How to tenderize, 129

Roast Chicken with Citrus, 63

Roast Chicken with Garlic, 62

Roast Turkey, 74

Roasted Beet Salad, 36

Roasted Butternut Squash, 103

Roasted Cauliflower with Olives, 104

Roasted Potatoes, 124

Roasted Tomatoes, 105

Rosemary Garlic Prawns, 88

Salads, 29

Salmon,
    Baked Lemon Salmon, 82
    Grilled Salmon, 83
    How to score, 83
    Salmon in White Wine, 89
    Salmon with Garlic Paste, 90
    Seafood Cobb Salad, 37
    Seafood Stew, 48
    Smoked Salmon Spread, 18
    Soy-Ginger Salmon, 93

Salmon in White Wine, 89

Salmon with Garlic Paste, 90

Sauces, 113

Sauerkraut,
    Pork Roast with Sauerkraut, 55

Sausage,
    Joe's Special, 67
    One-Pot Italian Sausage and Potatoes, 71
    Stuffed Mushrooms, 20
    Stuffed Red Peppers, 76

Sautéed Beet Greens, 106

INDEX

Scalloped Potatoes, 125

Scallops,
    Sea Scallops with Lime, 91
    Seafood Stew, 48

Sea Scallops with Lime, 91

Seafood Cobb Salad, 37

Seafood, 81

Seafood Stew, 48

Secret Sauce, 116

Sesame Spinach, 107

Shrimp Corkscrew Salad, 38

Shrimp Dip, 17

Shrimp,
    Chinese Egg Noodles with Shrimp, 33
    Shrimp Dip, 17
    Seafood Cobb Salad, 37
    Seafood Stew, 48
    Shrimp Corkscrew Salad, 38

Sides, 119

Slow Cooker, 51

Smoked Salmon Spread, 18

Sole with Capers and Olives, 92

Soy-Ginger Salmon, 93

Soups, 43

Soup Stock,
    Chicken Stock, 45

Sour Cream Sauce with Capers, 117

Southwest Chicken Chili, 53

Spelt flour, 23, 24, 25, 27

Spinach,
    Black-Eyed Peas, 121
    Chicken Noodle Soup, 44
    Joe's Special, 67
    Marinara Sauce, 69
    Minestrone Soup, 46
    One-Pot Italian Sausage and Potatoes, 71
    Sesame Spinach, 107
    Spinach Salad with Chicken, 39
    Spinach with Balsamic Vinegar, 108
    Strawberry Spinach Salad, 40

Spinach Salad with Chicken, 39

Spinach with Balsamic Vinegar, 108

Squash,
    Acorn Squash, 96
    Roasted Butternut Squash, 103

Steamed Clams with Pesto Sauce, 19

Strawberry Spinach Salad, 40

Stock, Chicken, 45

Stuffed Mushrooms, 20

Stuffed Red Peppers, 76

Stuffing, see dressing

Swedish Meatballs, 77

Sweet Corn Bread, 26

Sweet Potato Casserole, 126

Sweet Potato Salad, 35

Swiss Chard, 109

INDEX

Taco Salad, 41

Tartar Sauce, 118

Temperature, meat, 63

Tilapia with Rosemary-Ginger Rub, 94

Toasted Walnuts, 36

Tomato Basil Soup, 50

Tomatoes,
    Bruschetta, 15
    Caprese Chop Salad, 31
    Chicken with Fresh Mozzarella
        and Noodles, 58
    Chili, 59
    Deseeding, 15
    Italian Zucchini Bake, 101
    Marinara Sauce, 69
    Minestrone Soup, 46
    One-Pot Italian Sausage and Potatoes, 71
    Roasted Tomatoes, 105
    Seafood Stew, 48
    Spinach Salad with Chicken, 39
    Tomato Basil Soup, 50
    White Beans with Rosemary, 128

Turkey,
    Chili, 59
    Hamburgers — Mary's Style, 64
    Italian Meatballs, 66
    Joe's Special, 67
    Roast Turkey, 74
    Roasting times, 74
    Swedish Meatballs, 77
    Taco Salad, 41
    Turkey Meatloaf, 79

Turkey Meatloaf, 79

Twice-Baked Potatoes, 127

Vegetable Stir Fry, 110

Vegetables, 95

Vinaigrette, 42

Walnuts, how to toast, 22

Wild Blackberry Cobbler, 141

Wine,
    Caramelized Mushrooms in
        White Wine, 98
    Irish Lamb Stew, 54
    Pumpkin Soup, 47
    Salmon in White Wine, 89
    Seafood Stew, 48
    White Beans with Rosemary, 128

Yogurt Dipping Sauce, 118
    Artichokes with Yogurt Dipping Sauce, 97

Zucchini,
    Joe's Special, 67
    Italian Zucchini Bake, 101
    Zucchini Carrot Bread, 27
    Zucchini and Green Chiles, 111
    Zucchini Stir Fry, 112

Zucchini Carrot Bread, 27

Zucchini and Green Chiles, 111

Zucchini Stir Fry, 112

ORDER FORM

If you would like to order additional copies of this book, please fill out and mail me this order form.

Healthy Family Favorites

Please send _____ copies @ **$16.95 each** =

Shipping and handling:
- ☐ 1 book .... + **$4.00**
- ☐ 2-4 books .... + **$6.00**
- ☐ 5-10 books .... + **$8.00**

TOTAL

Mail books to:

Name _____

Address _____

City, State, Zip _____

Allow 2 weeks for delivery

Mail this form with your check to:

Mac Enterprises
P.O. Box 308
Kirkland, Washington 98083-0308
macplaid@yahoo.com